FREEDOM
FROM
FINANCIAL BONDAGE

How To Overcome Financial Frustration
and Walk in God's Supernatural Provisions

A Biblical Guide for Managing Money & Possessions

To: Michele Arrone

From: Frederick Esters

May God's Blessings
always be with You. 4/8/97

FREEDOM FROM FINANCIAL BONDAGE

How To Overcome Financial Frustration and Walk in God's Supernatural Provisions

A Biblical Guide for Managing Money & Possessions

by
Dwight Nichols

Harrison House
Tulsa, Oklahoma

Second Printing
Over 20,000 in Print

Freedom From Financial Bondage
How To Overcome Financial Frustration
and Walk in God's Supernatural Provisions
A Biblical Guide for Managing Money & Possessions
ISBN 0-89274-797-8
Copyright © 1995 by Dwight Nichols
Urban Impact Ministries
P. O. Box 901
North Little Rock, Arkansas 72115

Published by Harrison House, Inc.
P. O. Box 35035
Tulsa, Oklahoma 74153

CONTENTS

FIGURES

TABLES

DEDICATION

This book is dedicated to my wife, Cynthia, and my mother and father, Josephine and Conrad Nichols. Without their love, support and guidance over the years, I would never have made it to this point in my life.

I would also like to dedicate this book to my children, Trina, Dewayne and Christina in whom I am well pleased. My prayer for them is that the wisdom of God outlined in these pages will continue to serve as a guide for their lives, and that they will pass these principles on to their families so that their lives will be a living testimony of the goodness of God's provisions for generations to come.

ACKNOWLEDGMENTS

Iwould like to personally take the time to express my appreciation and thanks to Janice Drennan, who went above and beyond the call of duty in assisting me in every aspect of organizing this book, from layout and typesetting to final proofing for the publisher. She made a substantial contribution of her time and resources for the completion of this project.

Appreciation must be extended to Joyce Wilkerson, who volunteered her time and professional expertise in typesetting and layout for the workbook used in our Stewardship in Action — Small Group Study Course.

Special appreciation also goes to Pastor Happy Caldwell, Remo Jacuzzi, Pastor Silas Johnson, and my brothers, Richard and Larry Nichols, for their encouragement, inspiration and contribution of time and resources. I further thank Debbie Warrenton, who not only provided the dictating and typing skills to initiate this project, but who also has assisted me in many other projects over the past 12 years.

Last, but not least, I would like to express special appreciation for my business partner, Don Chastek, who has provided support and encouragement for this and many other projects. His practical wisdom and realistic feedback has been a stabilizing factor in my life.

FOREWORD

God has a financial system. The basic principle outlined in this book is the foundation for Godly prosperity, and if it is overlooked, it can cause frustration, wrong motives and abuse. Without being established in the "purpose" for prosperity, we can become motivated by greed, personal gain and self preservation.

The Bible is very clear that God gives us "power" (ability) to get wealth so He can establish His covenant in the earth — through us. However, I have seen many saints become disillusioned or complacent after being "motivated" to give, but not seeing their financial dreams realized.

It is not that the Word doesn't work, or that God doesn't want them to prosper. It is simply that they have no knowledge of the basic principles of biblical economics. Even if they did have temporary prosperity, it would be short lived.

Economics is stewardship. It is the science or study of how people make common-sense decisions regarding money: managing, investing and creating wealth. An economy by definition is the "management" of the resources of a household, business, city or government. There is no better type of economy than capitalism or free enterprise. Socialism, which our government is pushing us toward today, is the midway mark between capitalism and communism. Communism breeds humanism and totalitarianism. We know communism doesn't work. The Bible does not teach socialism but suggests free enterprise, where each individual has the right and responsibility to produce, save, invest and create wealth.

Communism was based on the belief that the universe was merely matter and energy and nothing else. This is materialism. If man is just a product of his environment, there is no God; then give him what he needs (food, clothing and shelter) and you can change human nature. False!

The Bible teaches that man and universe were created by God and, therefore, are both spiritual and material. Man was created in God's image and given dominion over His creation. Government and laws were vehicles by which God could offer protection to the innocent and punish the guilty. He taught man the basic principles of economics so that man could be a good steward over the wealth that He gave him the power and ability to produce.

There have been other books written about money management and finances. However, Dwight Nichols' approach is delightfully fresh and honest. Dwight has no hidden agendas. His motive is clear, and his purpose is to disciple the body of Christ in the use of biblical financial principles.

My favorite chapter is Chapter 6 on "Honesty and Integrity." I have never seen this area covered in money management, but it is the foundation of all God's blessings.

Freedom from Financial Bondage, if applied in faith, will change your life.

Happy Caldwell
Pastor, Agape Church, Little Rock, Arkansas

PREFACE
PRISONS WITHOUT WALLS:
REPAIRING BROKEN DREAMS

I was born in rural Alabama, the oldest of ten children of Conrad, Sr., and Josephine Nichols. I grew up in Prichard, Alabama, which was the poorest city in the state and, according to statistics from the U.S. Department of Health and Human Services, one of the poorest cities in the nation. Without ever realizing it, like many others I was being programmed with certain attitudes and expectations that would keep me bound to a specific lifestyle.

As a child, I dreamed of growing up to be a successful and influential businessman, able to help my family and to reach out and help others. But after years of chasing the dream without seeing results, reality began to set in. I began to accept the thought that maybe I had been born into the wrong race and economic background. My family did not have any money; so I did not feel that I had the corresponding privileges. I didn't know anyone in my family who had been successful in business; so why should I expect any more?

I began to believe the reason I wasn't doing as well as I should was because someone else was keeping me down. It wasn't my fault. It was the government's, or maybe it was the environment in which I was reared.

Even though I had a college degree, I could not see myself expanding beyond the neighborhood where I grew up. I was so busy trying to make money for myself that I didn't have time for anyone else. Although I was still a young man, I was trapped behind an invisible wall and held captive by my own attitude that was being reinforced by a poverty mentality. I was hopelessly bound by the circumstances of life and controlled by limited thinking. Although the way out was there all the time, I was blind to its existence.

In 1978, I started attending a Bible study that included scriptures on personal finances. As a small businessman, I had never recognized the Bible as a credible source for financial direction. I had been taught that it was irreverent to talk about money in church and that God was only interested in spiritual things. Nevertheless, I was so impacted by what I learned that I started an exhaustive study on my own. What I found changed the course of my life!

I began to realize God has a financial system already in place and the Bible outlines the plan for operating in His system. The Scripture has much to say about how to use money properly. In fact, 16 of the 38 parables that Jesus gave in the New Testament were concerned with how to handle money and possessions. As I continued to search the Scriptures, it was like a veil was lifted from my eyes. I began to realize that God didn't have a problem with Christians having money. In fact, I could see that God's financial plan for our lives was well above the expectations of the average Christian. I began to realize that I had been programmed with a poverty mentality that was not from God. I was locked into a certain lifestyle and limited by my own attitude and expectations.

Suddenly. as if a light had been turned on, I began to see beyond the walls that had me locked in! As I continued to study the Scripture, I began to think that it was possible to do what God's Word said I could do and that I could have what God said I could have financially. I began to realize that God was interested in my financial success, but I had to do my part in order for God to do His part. The principles that were developing before my eyes were so basic that I could not understand why I had never seen them on my own.

I could now see the mistakes I had made and the steps that should be taken to correct them. Because I took the time to learn the fundamental principles of how God's financial system works, God began to bless my finances.

As a result of applying these principles, although it took diligence and hard work, I was able to break the spirit of poverty that controlled my life.

From the moment I made the commitment to live by the Bible's principles of prosperity, my life has been an adventure. However, this was not the end of the story. Just as I thought everything was going well, I began to realize that something else was missing!

In 1989, God began to stir something inside me. Although I thought I was doing fine, God began to show me that I was falling well short of His mark. He began to direct my attention to the overall economic decay that was occurring around me. I could see the broken lives and broken dreams. People were caught in the clutches of poverty with no way out. I saw people with God-given potential being swept away by a tidal wave of economic circumstances beyond their control. I began to experience the hopelessness and despair in the eyes of others. My heart began to burst within my chest with compassion.

As I began to think back, God began to give me a broader perspective. I began to see that all the devastation and decay happening in our urban neighborhoods was caused by the same spirit of poverty that had controlled my life just a few years before. God reminded me that it was because someone had taken the time to share the biblical principles of prosperity with me that the economic direction of my life had changed.

As God brought these things to my consciousness, I began to realize that everything that I had done to this point was completely selfish and had no spiritual reward. I had moved from one trap to another. Instead of running just to make a living for my family ,now I was running to hold on to all the trappings of success without considering what was happening in the lives around me. All my efforts were focused toward myself, having no impact for the kingdom of God. I struggled with God on this issue. "What can I do that would have any type of impact on all this devastation?

I am only one person. It is hard enough just taking care of my own circumstances," I argued with myself and God.

"Father, I realize these principles changed my life, but I don't have the time," I continued. "There are only so many hours in the day." I reminded God that it took years of trial and error for me to move from where I was financially in the past to where I was at that point.

I continued to tell God that people are more interested in quick fixes than in long-term solutions. Although the principles are simple and straightforward, most people are not willing to make the commitment or take the time and effort to learn the principles of financial success and then have the discipline to apply them to their lives.

God reminded me this decision was not mine to make. Every individual would have to make the decision for himself or herself. What God wanted me to do was to be obedient to share how He had delivered me from the spirit of poverty, how these principles had changed my attitude and the financial circumstances in my life. God told me to tell as many people as I could that the same principles which transformed my life would transform theirs, if they were willing to learn them and diligently apply them to their circumstances, no matter what their race or economic background. God said, "If you are willing to take a step of faith and write down these principles as I have revealed them to you and then share them with others, I will do the rest."

In 1990, I made a decision to take two years off from the investment banking business to organize these principles into book form. In addition, I also developed the Stewardship in Action — Small Group Study Course, a 12-week study in Personal Finances. Together these two can be used as tools by churches and small groups who are serious about having an economic impact in the lives of individuals and thus impact the community they serve.

God has been faithful to His Word as pastors across the country have shown an interest in using this material to teach these principles of biblical stewardship to everyone in their congregations. More importantly, I see more and more pastors beginning to make the connection between being a good steward over economic matters and being a good steward over spiritual matters. They are beginning to realize that by teaching individuals to break the spirit of poverty and to impact their economic circumstances, the church is indirectly affecting the economic condition of the larger community it serves.

Moreover, with my spiritual eyes I see more churches starting to get serious about teaching the fundamentals of how to live successful lives and how to be good stewards and efficient money managers. As churches accept this aspect of their responsibility, I see people breaking free from the spirit of poverty and being able to come off welfare. I see those not directly caught in the downward economic spiral of our urban neighborhoods also becoming more effective managers of their resources. They are getting their financial houses in order so they will be in a position to reach out and extend a helping hand to others and have an impact for the kingdom of God.

My prayer for you is that as you read this book, God will give you a revelation of His financial system and the steps you can take to get your financial house in order. And, just as important to the body of Christ, as you get your finances under control, my prayer is that you will reach out and share these principles with at least two other families. The best way to share these principles is by letting people see them in operation in your life. Then invite them to attend a Stewardship in Action — Small Group Study Course at your local church. There is a special training session available to church leaders who want to establish a small group study course. (For more information about Stewardship in Action, write Urban Impact Ministries, P.O. Box 901, North Little Rock, AR 72115.)

If everyone who understands God's economic system did their part to apply it to their lives and then reached out to share these principles with others, together we could have an impact for the body of Christ and change the economic direction of our urban neighborhoods. We could be God's instrument for repairing broken dreams.

INTRODUCTION

The years ahead will see many turbulent economic changes, but I believe the church will witness the best opportunity in its history for the harvesting of souls for the kingdom of God. Although many will be swept away by economic calamity, those who understand the principles that govern God's economic system and are found faithful in applying these principles to their lives will flourish in the midst of chaos. They will have the financial resources to meet this challenge.

According to Deuteronomy 8:18, God has given each Christian the power to get wealth so that He might establish His covenant in the earth. Establishing His covenant in the earth is part of our economic destiny.

God has placed within every individual the ability to take control of their personal finances, to live successful lives and to make a positive contribution to society. However, by the time most become young adults, they have been programmed by a system that strives to keep them from reaching their full economic potential. Many will be completely controlled by the spirit of poverty. Their minds will have been programmed in such a way that it will keep them in financial bondage for the rest of their lives.

God wants to raise up individuals within the body of Christ who can be trusted with money. He wants us to get our financial houses in order, not only to meet our needs, but so that we will be able to reach out to those around us. He wants us to be in a position to give so that His covenant might be established on earth.

This will never happen in our lives unless we learn how to become good stewards over the money and resources that already have been entrusted to our care. Statistics say as much as two-thirds of our population will have to depend on the government to live after retirement. A record number of individuals are already on welfare or some form of government assistance. Moreover, an even greater number of families are struggling to survive from paycheck to paycheck. Bad credit records and personal bankruptcies have become commonplace. More disturbing yet, our urban areas are deteriorating at an alarming rate. The spirit of poverty has been allowed to imprison our inner cities with an attitude that stifles creativity and discourages economic progress on an individual basis.

As disappointing as it may seem, evidence suggests that there is not much difference between the Christian and non-Christian as it relates to personal finances. Because of the Madison Avenue mentality, even many Christians find themselves caught in the same "financial bondage" as the rest of the world. God cannot trust these Christians with larger amounts of money because they are not faithful with what they already have.

For those Christians who are willing to pay the price to learn how to handle money according to His guidelines, God will give supernatural abilities to receive worldly wealth. Yes, God is interested in our financial well-being. He wants to restore our families and rebuild our communities, but this can only be done on an individual-by-individual basis. We cannot depend on the government to do it. As the main economic unit of our society, families must learn how to assume the role that God originally intended. As Christians, we must be willing to accept our responsibility as stewards if we are going to walk victoriously in God's supernatural provision.

PURPOSE

Freedom from Financial Bondage will help you identify the principles that govern God's financial system. The main purpose of the book is to establish the fundamentals needed to become skillful managers of God's resources and to create and build wealth in God's economy.

Chapters 1-4 establish the basic issues of what God's attitude is about money and possessions. They examine what it means to be a good steward. These chapters identify fundamental reasons why the average family is struggling with their finances. They identify the principles that must be in place to build a solid foundation to receive God's financial blessing.

Chapters 5-10 examine principles that will help you multiply the amount of money you have to manage as a steward. In Deuteronomy 28, the Bible teaches that the blessings of God will overtake the individual who obeys these laws as they relate to money. These chapters outline those principles and relate things you can do yourself to bring financial increase.

Chapter 11 deals with faith for God's supernatural increase. Chapter 12 is the most practical of all. It outlines a 21-step action plan to "jump-start" your personal finances. The "21 Practical Steps to Build Wealth in God's Economy" are at the core of the related Stewardship in Action — Small Group Study Course — and outline the specific strategies necessary to get your financial house in order. Chapter 12 outlines a step-by-step plan with "action steps" that every individual should take to build a solid financial foundation.

God wants to take the struggle out of your personal finances. By learning these principles and applying them to your everyday life, you will be prepared to receive God's supernatural increase. No matter what happens in the world economy, and no matter what your current financial condition, you will be standing on solid ground.

This writer has a desire to see the local church become a strong economic force within the community that it serves. The principles outlined in God's Word can break the spirit of poverty and change the entire economic direction of a community. As each church teaches its members the basic principles of biblical economics and trains individuals within the church to teach these principles to others, it can begin to have significant impact within their communities. Only as we get our economic house in order can we reach out and extend a helping hand to those around us.

I am asking each individual who reads this book to make a firm commitment to walk in financial integrity and have a greater impact for God. See THE COMMITMENT, on page 197.

1

YOUR ECONOMIC DESTINY

GOD'S PLAN FOR YOUR LIFE

But thou shalt remember the Lord thy God: for it is He that giveth thee power to get wealth, that He may establish His covenant which He sware unto thy fathers, as it is this day.

Deuteronomy 8:18

I have been young, and now am old, yet have I not seen the righteous forsaken, nor his seed begging bread.

Psalm 37:25

Jan is a 27-year-old single parent with two children and a full-time job. She said she cannot live on her present salary.

"Well, what have you done to change your financial circumstances? Have you asked God to give you a creative idea?" I asked.

She said that she had been praying about the situation for a number of years, with no change in her circumstances, and that she was waiting for God to intervene on her behalf.

"Tell me, do you have any kind of plan to budget your spending? Do you set aside any portion of your current income for savings?" I continued.

"I don't earn enough money to worry about a budget or much less any kind of savings," she answered.

Jan is a committed Christian and genuinely loves the Lord. Nevertheless, she is trapped by the system and cannot see a way out. She even has a desire to give a portion of her income to the church, but she never seems to have enough left over after paying her bills.

Jan wants her financial circumstances to change, but has not put forth any specific action that would better her financial condition. Additionally, she has not properly managed what she already has. She has fallen into the same economic mindset as many Christians. She feels that if God wanted her to have more money, He would change her financial circumstances.

If Jan continues on her current path, she will never be free from the bondage of a poverty spirit. She will never achieve her full economic potential. She is halting progress toward her economic destiny without ever realizing it! What has she done to get in this position? Is there anything she can do to change her financial circumstances?

SATAN'S DECEPTION

The first and most important principle governing God's financial system is to have a proper understanding of God's attitude about money and wealth. The following scriptures tell us something about God's attitude:

> *But thou shalt remember the Lord thy God: for it is He that giveth thee the power to get wealth, that He may establish His covenant which He sware unto thy fathers, as it is this day.*

> Deuteronomy 8:18

> *The wealth of the sinner is laid up for the just.*

> Proverbs 13:22

God does not have a problem with Christians having money as long as the money does not control them. In fact, this is part of our economic destiny. If these scriptures are true, why aren't Christians walking in their provisions? Furthermore, why is it so many Christians who sincerely love the Lord are struggling to survive from paycheck to paycheck? Does Scripture suggest that we are supposed to receive certain financial blessings if we are committed Christians or give to God's work?

There are major misconceptions within the body of Christ, leading Christians to believe that God can take care of all of our financial problems with the wave of His hand without regard to the guidelines He has already given in His Word. These misconceptions prevent many Christians from receiving God's supernatural blessing in their lives.

Satan has been able to deceive many Christians into having the wrong attitude about money. They think that money is evil and that Christians are not supposed to care about it or have anything to do with it. This, of course, is a paradox in itself, because it takes money to live. Nevertheless, many Christians have been led to believe that there is something inherently spiritual about being poor. Some even feel that there is something wrong with being successful financially.

Other Christians feel they don't have any control over their financial circumstances; so why should they bother themselves with such matters? What will be will be. This is not what the Bible teaches. The truth of the matter is that God has provided an economic legacy for His children, but we must do our part to inherit what is rightfully ours.

OUR ECONOMIC HERITAGE — GOD'S SUPERNATURAL PROVISIONS

The perimeters of our economic inheritance have already been determined. We are to be blessed so that we can be a blessing. Deuteronomy 28 states that if we *listen diligently* to the voice of the Lord and *obey* His principles, the blessings of God will "come on thee and overtake thee." The blessings are automatic if we are obedient and follow God's instructions.

Our economic heritage is much broader than just paying bills and meeting our needs. It is not just money. It is an attitude that causes us to understand the true purpose and use of money — how to establish a sound financial base for our families, and yet be able to reach out and extend a helping hand to others. This economic inheritance has already been established, the legal parameters set and the conditions outlined in His Word. The rest is up to us!

WHY ARE THE RICH GETTING RICHER AND THE POOR GETTING POORER?

During the time I was working in the investment banking and securities industry, dealing with both wealthy individuals and institutional accounts, I made an important discovery: Some people continue to make money regardless of the condition of the economy or whether the market goes up or down.

This seemed unfair to me, that the people having the most money appeared to be getting more money, while the people who needed money were doing without. So I asked God this question: "Why are the rich getting richer and the poor getting poorer?"

One day while I was studying the Bible and meditating on His Word, God began to reveal the answer: He has put certain principles into operation on earth regarding money, and they will work for whoever uses them. When it rains, it rains on the just and unjust alike. The better you manage your money, the more money comes your way. Conversely, if you don't manage it properly, the money that you do have will never be enough. It will be taken away from you. This principle is documented throughout the Bible, but perhaps the most graphic illustration is in the following Scripture:

Take therefore the talent [money] from him, and give it unto him which hath ten talents. For unto everyone that hath shall be given, and he shall have abundance; but from him that hath not shall be taken away even that which he hath. And cast ye the unprofitable servant into outer darkness.

Matthew 25:28-30

4

Notice the money was taken away from the one who had the least and given to the one who had the most — the one who got the best results from what had already been entrusted to his care. The one who demonstrated through past actions that he knew how to get the best return was given that which was taken away from the one who had the least. It is what we do with what we have that gets God's attention!

The rich are getting richer because they understand the fundamental principles that govern wealth and manage these principles in their favor. The laws that govern wealth have already been set. On the other hand, the poor are getting poorer because they do not understand how to properly manage what they have; therefore, what they have will be taken away from them.

Like Jan, many Christians are trapped in economic bondage because of the wrong attitudes. They are waiting for God to perform a miracle to turn their finances around when the means are already within their reach. In fact, God has already made the provisions regarding their financial circumstances. But, because they think they don't have any control over their financial destiny, they don't properly take advantage of the provisions already provided them. In essence, they have thus locked God out of working in their financial circumstances.

MYTHS AND RELIGIOUS TRADITIONS

Our money is important to God, because it can be a powerful tool in the hands of faithful Christians. Because of the impact that this revelation can have for the kingdom of God and the powerful blow it can deliver to the kingdom of darkness, Satan has gone to great lengths to keep the church confused regarding the role of money in the life of a believer.

Through myths and religious traditions, Satan has been very successful in keeping us confused regarding our economic destiny. We have been programmed to have the wrong attitude about money. Satan has provided a steady flow of partial truths mixed with distortions in order to keep us confused in the areas of proper money management.

These myths and religious traditions surface in many forms. Many times they are different from one cultural and economic background to another. See if you can recognize any of these fables:

1. Money is the root of all evil; therefore, as committed Christians, you should not be concerned with savings or investments.

2. "I'm as poor as old Job's turkey (hen)." Poverty is a sign of spirituality. Christians are supposed to be poor to show their spirituality. To be spiritual, Christians must act as if they don't care about money.

3. It is easier for a camel to go through the eye of a needle than it is for a rich person to go to heaven; therefore, you can't have treasures on earth and expect to go to heaven too. It is wrong for you to build wealth and financial resources while here on earth.

4. Since money is a part of the world's economic system, and you are supposed to be heavenly minded, you should not talk about money in church. Or, "All preachers want to do is to get your money." The church is not the place for that sort of thing. The church's purpose is for worship of God, and it should stay out of people's business.

5. Jesus told the rich young ruler to sell his possessions and give his money away; therefore, if you love Jesus, you aren't supposed to have riches on earth. You will get your riches when you get to heaven.

6. If you really trust in Jesus and use faith, He will meet all your financial needs without your having to do anything about your circumstances.

7. God answers prayer; therefore, you don't have to plan ahead — just pray and take one day at a time. God will take care of you. You don't need to make preparations for the future.

8. God is interested only in spiritual things and not the mundane material things of everyday life.

9. Money is corrupt. It will lead you astray. If a person has money, that person must be stealing from someone.

10. Because a person tithes or gives to the Gospel, God is automatically bound to meet all of that person's financial needs without following the other principles that govern money as outlined in the Bible.

At the core of every myth is always a distorted biblical principle. Many of our attitudes about God's provisions are distorted because of misinformation. On the surface, these fables may sound humorous — or even religious. Even though none of the above myths are true, they grip the very heart and soul of Christians and non-Christians alike. These traditions are responsible for robbing us of our economic inheritance. As a result of these misrepresentations, many Christians don't feel comfortable even talking about money in church.

One of the primary purposes of *Freedom from Financial Bondage* is to dispel these myths by shining the light of God's Word on these misconceptions. God has outlined principles in His Word that would allow us as Christians to avoid the typical scenario that holds the average family hostage. By applying these guidelines to our personal finances, we can take the struggle out of our financial lives. By applying the basic fundamentals of biblical stewardship to our own personal finances, Christians can overcome the obstacles that are keeping them in financial bondage.

LACK OF KNOWLEDGE

Another reason many Christians are having difficulties with their personal finances is lack of knowledge about the Word:

My people are destroyed for lack of knowledge.

Hosea 4:6

This is certainly true when it comes to our personal finances. Because of the lack of proper biblical instruction in the area of God's way of handling money, Christians have had to resort to the same type of financial irresponsibility as the unsaved world. It is the lack of knowledge that over the years has allowed Satan to be so effective in his deceptive practices to pervert God's original intent about the use of money in the lives of Christians.

And he said, I am Abraham's servant. And the Lord hath blessed my master greatly; and he is become great: and He hath given him flocks, and herds, and silver, and gold, and menservants, and maidservants, and camels, and asses.

Genesis 24:34-35

Beloved, I wish above all things that thou mayest prosper and be in health, even as thy soul prospereth.

III John 2

Knowledge and understanding go hand in hand. Even if you had the knowledge of these two scriptures and were deceived into thinking that for some reason they were not true, or if you did not have the understanding of how to apply them to your financial circumstances, they would be of no benefit. This part of your biblical inheritance would have no effect on your life. It would have no significance on your financial destiny unless you knew how to embrace it.

Beyond knowledge, there is another step that must be taken. Once you learn the Word of God, you must be willing to act and apply it to your life.

NATURAL ACTS DETERMINE SPIRITUAL BENEFITS

Now that we know that there are certain things we must do to prepare ourselves to receive the benefits of God's provisions, let's take a closer look at action and what the long-term spiritual benefits are.

See if you can glean any significant insight from the following scriptures that might be helpful to us in this effort.

Let's examine the economic circumstances that existed with the widow in the following scripture:

And as she was going to fetch it, he called to her, and said, Bring me, I pray thee, a morsel of bread in thine hand. And she said, As the Lord thy God liveth, I have not a cake, but an handful of meal in a barrel, and a little oil in a cruse: and, behold, I am gathering two sticks, that I may go in and dress it for me and my son, that we may eat it, and die. And Elijah said unto her, Fear not; go and do as thou hast said: but make me thereof a little cake first, and bring it unto me, and after make for thee and for thy son. For thus saith the Lord God of Israel, The barrel of meal shall not waste, neither shall the cruse of oil fail, until the day that the Lord sendeth rain upon the earth. And she went and did according to the saying of Elijah: and she, and he, and her house, did eat many days. And the barrel of meal wasted not, neither did the cruse of oil fail, according to the word of the Lord, which He spake by Elijah.

I Kings 17:11-16

If we have a word from God that would change our economic conditions, how would we apply it to our lives? In this passage, we should remember that bad economic conditions were already in the land. The widow of Zarephath was down to a handful of meal when Elijah, the prophet, came to her. She had only enough left for one meal. But the woman's actions changed her circumstances.

By her obedience and faithfulness to do what the Word of God said through Elijah, she then had no lack, and her needs were met. Her circumstances changed!

If the widow had not obeyed Elijah, the prophet, she would not have received the blessings God had for her. She and her son would have died for lack of food. But by acting in obedience on the Word of God, she enabled God to turn

9

her whole situation from that of death to life. The same is true in our lives.

From these scriptures, we can see that we must not only know what the Word of God says, but we must also be obedient and act on the Word of God according to God's guidelines to receive the benefits.

But what are the actual spiritual rewards of faithfully acting on God's Word regarding our finances?

THE SPIRITUAL REWARDS

And he said unto him, Well, thou good servant: because thou hast been faithful in a very little, have thou authority over ten cities.

Luke 19:17

The Bible points out that there is a close correlation between skillful money management and spiritual things. This is also part of our economic inheritance. The above scripture points out that because the steward was faithful with money, he would be given authority over cities when the master returned to establish his kingdom.

Notice Jesus told this parable Himself. The reward for good stewardship includes a spiritual reward to be given when Jesus returns. He was using money to illustrate this kingdom principle. The people who are faithful with the Master's money here on earth will be given authority to rule when He returns.

If therefore ye have not been faithful in the unrighteous mammon, who will commit to your trust the true riches?

Luke 16:11

This scripture further illustrates that if you are not faithful with money, you won't be faithful with spiritual things.

Another scripture relating to money management follows:

His lord said unto him, Well done, thou good and faithful servant: thou hast been faithful over a few things, I will make thee ruler over many things: enter thou into the joy of thy Lord.

Matthew 25:21

In this scripture, the good and faithful steward, who was faithful with the master's money, would be given more over which to be faithful. However, in addition to receiving more money to manage, notice he also would be allowed to enter into the joy of the Lord.

In all of these scriptures, the stewards were rewarded for being faithful with money. Also notice that each one of these Scriptures describes a spiritual reward that would be received.

There is a close correlation between faithfulness in handling money and faithfulness in handling spiritual things. If you aren't faithful with unrighteous money, you won't be faithful with spiritual things.

Yet the majority of families have never been able to budget their spending. Many wander aimlessly through life without ever realizing God has attached an importance to material possessions.

CONCLUSION

In concluding this chapter, it is very important to realize that, first of all, we have an economic destiny. God has already made economic and financial provisions for His children. These provisions are available to us regardless of our financial condition or the condition of the economy. But because of a lack of knowledge and myths and traditions, many individuals, both Christian and non-Christian, don't realize how broad and nonrestrictive God's provisions are. We have been programmed to fail due to wrong attitudes.

It is also very important to realize how God wants Christians to be faithful with the resources He has entrusted to our care. He wants us to become skillful managers of worldly wealth so we can have a greater impact for the kingdom of God. He wants us to get our financial houses in order so that we can be in a position to reach out to others.

Finally, we have noted that to walk in the economic provision God has already provided, we must be obedient to act on His Word to receive the benefits. To survive and even prosper during turbulent economic times, we must understand that God wants us to be successful.

In the following chapters, you will find there are basic principles that govern God's financial system and that there are many principles outlined in the Bible that give us insight into various aspects of our personal finances. But none is more important than that of biblical stewardship, which we will discuss further in the next chapter.

PRACTICAL APPLICATION

The practical application exercises for this chapter are as follows:

1. See if you can name three religious traditions and myths that would adversely affect a Christian's attitude about money and personal possessions.

2. Read the listed scriptures and answer the following question: What will happen if you don't properly manage the money you have? (Matthew 25:28, Luke 16:1-2.)

3. Read I Kings 17:11-16 and answer the question: What does it take for a Christian to receive the benefits God has provided in His Word?

2

THE STEWARDSHIP PRINCIPLE

THE KEY TO SUCCESS WITH GOD

Moreover it is required in stewards, that a man be found faithful.

I Corinthians 4:2

Yours is the mighty power and glory and victory and majesty. Everything in the heavens and earth is yours, O Lord, and this is your kingdom. We adore you as being in control of everything. Riches and honor come from you alone, and you are the Ruler of all mankind; your hand controls power and might, and it is at your discretion that men are made great and given strength.

I Chronicles 29:11-12 (TLB)

Once Bob realized that things were not working out as he had anticipated with Sue going back to work, he decided to approach her about the problem. "Sue, we need to do something about these bills. I think that it's about time you stop spending all of our money on clothes. The credit card bill just came, and the charges are up again this month."

"Why didn't you think about that before you decided to buy that boat and fishing equipment?" Sue responded, "Yes, I used the charge card. I had to buy some better clothes for work. We're also spending more money on gas, lunches and day care for the kids now. Then there's the additional car note to pay every month."

Bob and Sue are having marital problems stemming from difficulties in managing their personal finances. Bob is the manager of a local hardware store. Over the past 15 years of marriage, Sue's main responsibility has been to care for their three children and manage the household.

Approximately nine months ago Bob encouraged Sue to take a job outside the home to earn extra money to buy a new car. Instead of improving the situation, however, her working seems to have caused more difficulties within the family. It appears that the family has less disposable income than before Sue started to work.

This is a typical story being retold thousands of times across the country. The average income earned by the typical American family, with both parents working, is between $30,000 and $40,000 per year. Nevertheless, many of these families live from paycheck to paycheck, spending everything they earn just to keep afloat. I've found couples earning $75,000 who could not live off what they earn. The more money they earn, the more money they tend to spend. They are in "financial bondage." They can't reach out to others because they are strapped themselves. The average American family is going in the hole by spending more than they earn without ever realizing it.

According to statistical data, many families are finding themselves in the same position as Bob and Sue. Even with both husband and wife working, families usually find their spending increasing faster than their income. After taxes and the expenses of working, they find themselves bringing home much less money than they expected.

The key to solving this dilemma of not having enough is to understand and apply biblical stewardship to your finances. It's not the amount you have but what you do with what you have. The stewardship principle is being faithful with what you have, starting where you are. As you demonstrate your faithfulness with small amounts of money, God will give you more. If you don't properly manage a small income, you won't be able to manage a larger income. Biblical stewardship is the key to success with God.

The key to wealth in God's financial system is to start where you are and use what you have. A good steward understands how money works and makes it work in his or her favor.

THE GOOD STEWARD

What does it really mean to be a good steward? True biblical stewardship as it relates to finances is one of the most misunderstood subjects in the Bible. Because of the importance of money in our lives, Satan has managed to distort our true purpose as it relates to managing personal resources.

The definition of a steward is a person who manages someone else's property on behalf of the owner. The most appropriate definition of stewardship is faithfully applying God's principles to everything with which you have been entrusted. Good stewardship is properly managing your time, abilities and money. It does not deal only with finances, nor does it deal only with spiritual matters. It covers everything; we will be judged in terms of what we've done with all the things that God has entrusted to our care — time, ability and resources.

In examining the stewardship principles outlined in Matthew 25:14-30, Luke 16:1-13 and Luke 19:12-30, we are able to get true biblical insight into what God had in mind when He said, "good and faithful servant" (a good and faithful steward). The good and faithful steward is one who manages money and resources according to the principles and guidelines God has outlined in His Word.

The good steward is a person who increases wealth and multiplies the resources on behalf of the master. The good steward is the person who is skillful and businesslike in handling monetary affairs. The good steward is one who is faithful and diligent in carrying out instructions given by the owner of the goods.

> *ACTION STEP:*
> *LEARN HOW TO CREATE WEALTH*
> *TO BENEFIT THE KINGDOM*

The biggest challenge to Christians is the revelation that we will only have control of these things for a short period of time, while we are here on earth. We are to use the money as God's agent for good on the earth. If we use all that we receive on ourselves, we have mismanaged God's resources.

YOU WILL BE JUDGED ON HOW YOU HANDLE MONEY

Why is it important for us as Christians to understand the stewardship principle? Because it is the foundation for all other spiritual principles, and it will affect our lives throughout eternity. You will be judged by your faithfulness with material things. The most important principle we learn as Christians is biblical stewardship. This principle covers everything that we do while we are here on earth:

> *For we must all appear before the judgment seat of Christ; that every one may receive the things done in his body, according to that he hath done, whether it be good or bad.*
>
> II Corinthians 5:10

> *Moreover it is required in stewards, that a man be found faithful.*
>
> I Corinthians 4:2

> *ACTION STEP:*
> *LEARN TO BE A FAITHFUL STEWARD*
> *OVER YOUR FINANCES*

If we are spending all we earn on ourselves, how can we benefit the kingdom of God? The most important step in taking control of our personal finances is to learn how to be a good and faithful steward. If we are going to be judged according to how we handle the things with which God has entrusted us here on earth, we should learn what God expects of us. We must know what God's part is and what our part is.

GOD'S PART

ACTION STEP:
RECOGNIZE THAT GOD IS OWNER

The first step to being a good steward is to recognize God as the owner of everything. He is the God of the Universe, Creator and Supreme Ruler over the earth and everything in the earth:

Thine, O Lord, is the greatness, and the power, and the glory, and the victory, and the majesty: for all that is in the heaven and in the earth is thine; thine is the kingdom, O Lord, and thou art exalted as head above all. Both riches and honour come of thee, and thou reignest over all; and in thine hand is power and might; and in thine hand it is to make great, and to give strength unto all.

I Chronicles 29:11-12

To develope the right attitude about our money and possessions, it is important to see the whole picture from an eternal perspective. As ruler and master, God is in control of everything on earth; and His ownership is everlasting:

The land shall not be sold for ever: for the land is mine; for ye are strangers and sojourners with me.

Leviticus 25:23

ACTION STEP:
DEVELOP THE RIGHT ATTITUDE
ABOUT MONEY AND POSSESSIONS

The right attitude is to realize that God is owner:

For every beast of the forest is mine, and the cattle upon a thousand hills. I know all the fowls of the mountains: and the wild beasts of the field are mine. If I were hungry, I would not tell thee: for the world is mine, and the fulness thereof.

Psalm 50:10-12

As owner, God sets the guidelines. He makes the rules. To properly manage our money and possessions, we must learn what God expects of us. Then we must conduct the affairs of our lives according to His expectations.

ACTION STEP:
LEARN WHAT GOD EXPECTS OF US

With God as owner, we must realize that we will have possessions only for a short period of time. When we pass on, all material possessions will remain on the earth:

For we brought nothing into this world, and it is certain we can carry nothing out.

I Timothy 6:7

Although we have temporary control, all these things will ultimately return to God.

OUR PART

The second step to being a good steward is to recognize that we have a role to play. What does it mean to be a good steward? The Bible teaches this principle:

His Lord said unto him, Well done, thou good and faithful servant: thou hast been faithful over a few things, I will make thee a ruler over many things: enter thou into the joy of thy Lord.

Matthew 25:21

What does it take to rule over many things? You must be found faithful with what you have. In examining the parable, we see that the master called his servants (or his stewards) to him and entrusted to them a certain amount of money. To one he gave five talents, to one he gave two talents, and to another he gave one talent. He gave them his money based on their ability. After he entrusted them with his resources, he left them in charge and took his journey, and he told them to do business until he returned.

ACTION STEP:
BE FAITHFUL WITH WHAT YOU ALREADY HAVE

What did the two stewards do to deserve this type of recognition from the master? They were faithful with the master's money. The first two stewards took their lord's money and doubled it, but the third steward took the money and buried it in the ground. To the first two servants, the master said:

Well done, thou good and faithful servant:... enter into the joy of thy Lord.

Matthew 25:21

To the servant who buried his money, the master said:

Thou wicked and slothful servant, thou knewest that I reap where I sowed not, and gather where I have not strawed. Thou oughtest therefore to have put my money to the exchangers [banks], and then at my coming I should have received mine own with usury [interest]. Take therefore the talent [money] from him, and give it unto him which hath ten talents. For unto every one that hath shall be given, and

19

he shall have abundance: but from him that hath not shall be taken away even that which he hath. And cast ye the unprofitable servant into outer darkness: there shall be weeping and gnashing of teeth.

Matthew 25:26-30

Both of the faithful stewards doubled the money the master had given them and were given the reward. But notice that the money was taken from the third one, who had done the least. Likewise, the better you manage the money with which you have been entrusted, the more money you will have to manage.

WHAT ABOUT THE OTHER 90 PERCENT?

The stewardship principle as it relates to personal finances means being faithful with all of the money that's been entrusted to you — the whole dollar, not just part.

ACTION STEP:
LEARN HOW TO MANAGE THE OTHER 90 PERCENT

The stewardship principle covers more than just the 10 percent for tithes. As we take a look at stewardship, we are to realize that God is interested in what we do with the other part as well.

Figure 1
100%
GOD IS INTERESTED IN THE WHOLE DOLLAR

90%
After Tithe

10%
Tithe

Unfortunately, many Christians believe stewardship ends after they have given tithes or offerings on Sunday morning. Then they go into the rest of the week and deal with the balance of their finances pretty much as the rest of the world does. After leaving church, they are using the same concepts and the same principles as the unsaved world. The Bible describes this as the world system:

And be not conformed to this world: but be ye transformed by the renewing of your mind.

Romans 12:2

Many Christians are conforming to the world system without realizing it. Basically, God wants us to learn His principles (not those of the world) and apply them to all our personal possessions, including the remaining 90%.

ACTION STEP:
REALIZE EVERYTHING WE OWN
WHILE WE ARE HERE ON EARTH
WILL REMAIN ON EARTH

This is a fundamental principle that God wants to get across to us. In I Timothy 6:17-19, the Scripture states that the gold, silver, resources and fruits of our labor will remain in the earth and that they will do good or evil based only on the person in control of them. If we, as Christians, are in control of the resources, we can use these resources to benefit the kingdom of God.

BIBLICAL PRIORITIES

What are the priorities that God outlines in His Word regarding our personal finances?

But seek ye first the kingdom of God, and His righteousness; and all these things will be added unto you.

Matthew 6:33

Our first priority, then, is our individual relationship with God. The vertical relationship must be strong before we can be successful in other relationships. Every other activity is secondary. We must always seek God and His righteousness first.

ACTION STEP:
GET YOUR PRIORITIES IN THE PROPER ORDER

Everything Jesus discussed while He was here on earth focused on our relationship with God the Father. Everything else was a lower priority.

The second priority, after God, is our relationship with our families. Our main focus should be our immediate family: The relationship first between husband and wife, and secondly between parents and children. We should take care of our families and make sure our children understand the spiritual side of the Gospel. We should always point our children in the right direction:

Train up a child in the way he should go: and when he is old, he will not depart from it.

Proverbs 22:6

This principle will be discussed further in Chapter 10.

Finally, our third priority is our profession or business. The third priority takes into account how we earn a living, our professional and business activities. How we earn the money we have and what we are willing to do to get the money says a lot about our spiritual life.

First is God; second, family; and third, profession or business. We must always keep this in the right priority.

HOW TO RECEIVE MORE MONEY

God could give you one idea that could double, triple or otherwise multiply your income. But, according to the stewardship principle described in Matthew 25, if you didn't manage your money, it would cause you more harm than good.

If your income is small, how do you get more money? In examining the stewardship principle, our primary responsibility is to be faithful with what we have:

> *For unto every one that hath shall be given, and he shall have abundance: but from him that hath not shall be taken away even that which he hath.*

Matthew 25:29

ACTION STEP:
BE FAITHFUL WITH THE MONEY
WITH WHICH GOD HAS ENTRUSTED YOU;
LEARN HOW TO MAKE IT GROW

Being faithful with what we have is the key aspect of the stewardship principle as it relates to personal finances. Being faithful with what we have is the prerequisite for receiving more in the future. If we don't take care of the resources we have, God will not bless us with additional resources in the future.

The steward who was not faithful with what he had, had it taken away from him. Look back at the first part of Matthew 25:29:

> *For unto every one that hath shall be given.*

On close examination of this verse, we see that it could easily read, "For unto everyone who is faithful with what he has, it shall be given and that person shall have abundance, but from him who is not faithful with what he has, it shall be taken away even that which he has."

ACTION STEP:
IF YOU DON'T USE IT,
YOU WILL LOSE IT

This is part of the reason we see so much economic decay in our urban centers. Most people don't understand how to apply the basic principle of stewardship!

CONCLUSION

The only thing that will count for eternity is what we have done for the kingdom of God — how we have used the resources that God has provided to benefit the kingdom.

Yet too many Christians are living from day to day. They don't have anything left to help anyone else. They spend all of their working time trying to make a living for themselves and their families. They genuinely love God, but they are struggling just to make ends meet. They have to believe God for a miracle just to pay their electric bills.

Bob and Sue are members of a small church that reaches out to the community. They want to give more finances to the church, but because of their present financial situation, they don't have anything to give. They are using all the financial resources God has given on themselves. As a result, they are having no impact for His kingdom.

PRACTICAL APPLICATION

1. After reading this chapter, identify steps that you can take to be a more effective steward of the resources with which God has entrusted you.

In our Stewardship in Action — Small Group Study Course, we commit the following scripture to memory:

The earth is the Lord's, and the fulness thereof; the world, and they that dwell therein.

Psalm 24:1

This scripture reminds us that God is really the true owner of all things, and we are only the stewards of what He has given us.

2. If you are serious about getting your financial house in order, contact Urban Ministries to order the Stewardship in Action — Small Group Study Course.

3. Contact your pastor about attending the next Stewardship in Action — Small Group Study in your area. If one does not exist, ask him or her if it might be possible to establish one in your church.

Your success is based on how well you manage the Lord's property while you are here on earth.

3

PLANNING AND PREPARATION

WHAT TO DO WITH THE OTHER 90%

A prudent man foresees the difficulties ahead and prepares for them, the simpleton goes blindly on and suffers the consequences.

Proverbs 22:3 (TLB)

Any enterprise is built by wise planning, becomes strong through common sense, and profits wonderfully by keeping abreast of the facts.

Proverbs 24:3-4 (TLB)

But don't begin until you count the cost. For who would begin construction of a building without first getting estimates and then checking to see if he has enough money to pay the bills?

Luke 14:28 (TLB)

It had been approximately two years since John and Janet were shocked into reality. John had been laid off from his job which he had held for the past 25 years. His company had merged with another corporation, and as a result, John had lost his job.

John and Janet had thought that because this company had been around for 75 years, John had a secure job. With an annual bonus and profit-sharing, John realized he was receiving an annual salary well above what he could get on the current job market. It would be difficult for him to find a comparable position.

John had learned from his father that one should always put a "little something" aside for the future. Although he had put some savings in a mutual fund, over the years he and Janet became captured by the trappings of the good life. They had thought financial ruin could never happen to them. But due to the severity of their situation, they were forced to sell their home and drastically reduce their lifestyle.

Initially it was a disaster for Janet when they moved into an apartment. She had never thought they could survive on the $1,000 per month they had from a mutual fund investment. For the first time in their lives, they were forced to budget their income. They cut back on spending and set realistic priorities based on their current income. Their apartment utility bills were less than a third of what they had been paying. They conducted all spending on a cash basis. Fancy clothes, eating out and entertainment were eliminated. They sold most of their furniture. They took drastic measures to bring their expenses in line with their income — and realized they could live on much less than they thought.

John and Janet learned two basic principles of God's financial system: Always set aside a portion of your income and live within your means. They would eventually recover from the setback because they had set aside a portion of their income for emergencies and had enough discipline to drastically restructure their lifestyle. They realized that no job is forever in our economy, and they could live on a lot less money than they thought they could two years earlier.

FIRST THINGS FIRST

In order to take control of your personal finances and walk in God's financial provisions, you must plan ahead. Your first goal in becoming free from financial bondage is to learn how to develop a surplus. This process is easy once you learn how God's financial system operates. If you spend less than you take in, you will always have a surplus. What to do with this surplus will be discussed in greater detail in Chapter 8, which deals with saving and investing.

Many Christians feel that after they have given a tithe (10%) or offering, their spiritual responsibility is over as far as money is concerned. This is not what the Bible teaches. God is interested in how we handle the whole dollar, not just part. If you don't properly manage the other 90%, you will never have a surplus, and a steward without a surplus will always have financial problems. They are not properly managing their money and are wasting their resources by consuming everything to meet their own needs. They will never walk in the fullness of God's financial provisions.

As a steward, we are responsible for managing 100% of everything that has been entrusted to our care. We must revise our thinking to take into account that we are stewards over all the Lord's money. We will be held accountable if we waste God's resources.

And He said also unto His disciples, There was a certain rich man, which had a steward; and the same was accused unto him that he had wasted his goods. And he called him, and said unto him, How is it that I hear this of thee? Give an account of thy stewardship; for thou mayest be no longer steward.

Luke 16:1-2

This scripture points out the results of wasteful action, as it relates to money. Each Christian should be interested in getting as much mileage as possible from every dime of every dollar. With this in mind, as good stewards we must ask ourselves how we can plan our financial affairs, starting where we are, so that we will always have a financial surplus.

HOW TO DEVELOP YOUR FULL ECONOMIC POTENTIAL

A good steward knows how money works and plans for the future. Planning ahead helps you walk in your full economic potential. It allows you to prepare yourself to be able to meet the conditions that God has put forward in His Word. Once God tells you to do something in His Word, it is not always possible for you to do it right then. Planning ahead allows you to get into a position where you can be obedient to do what the Word of God tells you to do. This is especially true when it comes to your personal finances.

The purpose of this chapter is to help you organize a plan to manage the whole dollar so that you can get the maximum benefit from every dollar that God has entrusted to your care.

HOW TO BE A GOOD STEWARD OVER THE WHOLE DOLLAR

To take control of your finances, you must look at your total income from a different perspective. You must take control of each dollar and tell it which direction it should go. The first step is to develop a budget. Setting a budget will be examined in more detail later in this chapter. Notice the illustration below for outgoing expenditures as they relate to your budgetary dollar. This is the amount of money you have to spend each month.

Figure 2
OUTGOING EXPENDITURES
YOUR BUDGETARY DOLLAR

Most individuals spend 100% of their money without taking God into account. If every Christian gives 10% of their income to carry out the work of the Gospel, this would be represented by the 10% portion in Figure 2. The 90% portion of Figure 2 represents what they have left to cover other expenditures (living expenses). The 100% on the right of Figure 2 represents the total amount of income, the whole dollar.

Most Christians, once they give to God's work, return to the same practices as non-Christians to determine how they spend the balance of their money. For the most part, they are ending up with the same disastrous results.

GOD'S ATTITUDE ABOUT PLANNING AHEAD

Planning ahead allows us the ability to look into the future and see our desires. It helps us close the gap between hope and reality. It is the natural bridge that can carry us from where we are in the present to where God wants us to be in the future. Planning and preparation are fundamental principles outlined in the Bible, which will have a definite impact on your personal finances. Once we identify biblical guidelines for managing our finances, it is necessary for us to prepare a plan of action to accomplish our goals.

ACTION STEP:
REALIZE THAT GOD HAS ESTABLISHED
GUIDELINES THAT ALLOW YOU TO
PROPERLY PLAN YOUR FINANCIAL AFFAIRS,
NO MATTER HOW MUCH MONEY YOU EARN

There are many verses in the Bible that indicate we should plan our actions. Planning is key for success.

Any enterprise is built by wise planning, becomes strong through common sense, and profits wonderfully by keeping abreast of the facts.

Proverbs 24:3-5 (TLB)

Suppose one of you wants to build a tower. Will he not first sit down and estimate the cost to see if he has enough money to complete it?

Luke 14:28 (NIV)

Write the vision and make it plain upon tables, that he may run that readeth it.

Habakkuk 2:2

ACTION STEP:
ALWAYS PLAN YOUR FINANCIAL AFFAIRS —
DON'T ALLOW THEM TO HAPPEN HAPHAZARDLY

As we examine these scriptures, we should note that God planned ahead. He made preparations for the plan of salvation before He created the world. He looked forward into the future and saw Jesus crucified on the cross. Then He worked backward to establish steps with Jesus's obedience clearly in sight. God always plans ahead. Jesus told the disciples before He left that He was going to prepare a place for them in heaven. The scripture reads:

There are many homes up there where my Father lives, and I am going to prepare them for your coming. When everything is ready, then I will come and get you, so that you can always be with me where I am. If this weren't so, I would tell you plainly.

John 14:2-3 (TLB)

There are some other notable examples of planning and preparation in the Bible.

Noah was another who trusted God. When he heard God's warning about the future, Noah believed him even though there was then no sign of a flood, and wasting no time, he built the ark and saved his family. Noah's belief in God was in direct contrast to the sin and disbelief of the rest of the world — which refused to obey — and because of his faith he became one of those whom God has accepted.

Hebrews 11:7 (TLB)

Notice the sequence — a word from God, then Noah began to prepare in line with God's plan. Other examples are:

"Solomon my son is young and tender," David said, "and the Temple of the Lord must be a marvelous structure, famous and glorious throughout the world; so I will begin the preparations for it now." So David collected the construction materials before his death.

I Chronicles 22:5 (TLB)

Where there is no vision, the people perish: but he that keepeth the law, happy is he.

Proverbs 29:18

ACTION STEP:
TAKE CONTROL OF YOUR PERSONAL FINANCES BY PLANNING AHEAD

In I Corinthians 14:40, the Scripture states that things should be done decently and in order. Our God is a God of planning and organization.

Find some capable, godly, honest men who hate bribes, and appoint them as judges, one judge for each 1000 people; he in turn will have ten judges under him, each in charge of a hundred; and under each of them will be two judges, each responsible for the affairs of fifty people; and each of these will have five judges beneath him, each counseling ten persons.

Exodus 18:21 (TLB)

33

This home of mine shall be a tent pavilion — a Tabernacle. I will give you a drawing of the construction plan, and the details of each furnishing.

Exodus 25:9 (TLB)

Notice in both scriptures God was giving detailed instructions ahead of time for something He wanted to accomplish.

In those days was Hezekiah sick unto death. And the prophet Isaiah the son of Amoz came to him, and said unto him, Thus saith the Lord, Set thy house in order; for thou shalt die, and not live.

II Kings 20:1

We can see from these scriptures that King Hezekiah was instructed to plan for his death. A wise steward plans ahead.

HOW TO SUBSTANTIALLY INCREASE YOUR DISPOSABLE INCOME

Figure 3

WHERE IS YOUR DOLLAR GOING?

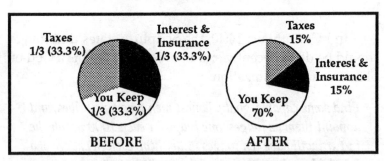

BEFORE   AFTER

This figure shows your income before and after applying biblical guidelines for managing money.

For the average family, each dollar can be divided roughly into three categories: 1/3 taxes, 1/3 interest and insurance and 1/3 which you keep, usually to pay debt and living expenses. Once the bills are paid, there is nothing left for emergencies or the things of God. (See Figure 2.)

By setting financial goals, establishing a budget and planning ahead, you can greatly increase your disposable income. (See Figure 3.) Our goal in this chapter is to examine the biblical principle of planning as it relates to reducing the categories that rob the average Christian of disposable income.

ACTION STEP:
ORGANIZE YOUR PLAN
ACCORDING TO BIBLICAL GUIDELINES

HOW TO LIVE ON 70%

This section will help us examine ways to allocate the other 90%. First of all, set a goal to live on 70% of your income. At first this might seem absolutely impossible, especially to those individuals who are having problems living on 100% of what they already earn.

Even though it may seem impossible, let's take a closer look at this concept. If you could realign current finances so that you only spent 70% of each paycheck, what would this do for your personal finances? First, you would put yourself in a position where you could systematically take into account every financial principle described in the Bible.

ACTION STEP:
SET YOUR FINANCIAL GOALS
ACCORDING TO BIBLICAL GUIDELINES

Joseph followed this basic pattern:

Let Pharaoh do this, and let him appoint officers over the land, and take up the fifth part of the land [20%] of Egypt in the seven plenteous years. And let them gather all the food of those good years that come, and lay up corn under

35

*the hand of Pharaoh, and let them keep food in the cities.
And that food shall be for store to the land against the seven
years of famine, which shall be in the land of Egypt; that the
land perish not through the famine.*

Genesis 41:34-36

Notice that Joseph recommended to Pharaoh that he take a fifth part, 20%, and set it aside. In other words, Joseph recommended that the Egyptians set aside 20% when the resources were coming in so that they would have resources when hard times came. Even though the Egyptians did not tithe, we know Joseph was a wise steward and understood the tithing principle.

The same pattern is evident in Proverbs 6. According to this scripture, the ants were wise because they set aside resources in the summer so that they would have provisions in the winter. This is not a biblical law, but it is a biblical pattern.

ACTION STEP:
SET A GOAL TO LIVE ON 70%

Second, if we set a goal of living on 70%, we would have a 30% surplus, including the first 10% to give to God's work. This would put God in first place.

And third, it would provide a steady source of revenue for your short-term and long-term savings accounts.

ACTION STEP:
ESTABLISH YOUR SAVINGS AND INVESTMENTS
TO BE CONSISTENT WITH THESE GUIDELINES

For example, if we set aside 10% for short-term savings, we would have a surplus account that could be used to extend a helping hand to those around us. We could give to the poor and needy and still have enough money to purchase the things we need. We would have enough resources to carry us through unforeseen emergencies, repairs, insurance deductibles or even to be able to pay cash for new purchases.

If we set aside 10%, for example, for long-term savings, we would be in a position to plan ahead for retirement. We wouldn't have to depend on the government when we retired. Compound interest would be working for us instead of us working for it. We would be in a position to lend and not borrow. According to Deuteronomy, we would be the head, not the tail.

NOTE: The 10% for long- and short-term savings is just an example and goal to shoot for. You may not be in a position to save this amount at the present time, but you should set aside something.

If we set living on 70% as a goal, it would change the entire complexion of our existing financial picture. Under this new arrangement, the outgoing expense chart would look like Figure 4.

Figure 4
OUTGOING EXPENDITURES
YOUR BUDGETARY DOLLAR

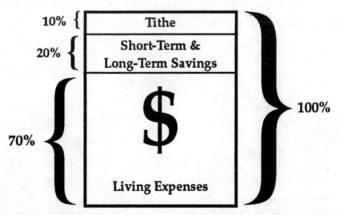

Figure 4 shows your budget with outgoing spending under control. By setting a goal to live on 70%, you have a 20% surplus.

If you set aside 30% of your income in a surplus account, you would have 70% to spend on monthly living expenses. This means you would automatically be living within your means because you would be forcing monthly expenditures to fit within the guidelines you established.

By setting a goal to live on 70%, you would manage the whole dollar, not just part. You would be in a position to live above the ups and downs in the economy. You wouldn't be at the mercy of your employer. You would never again have more month than money.

THE FAMILY BUDGET

With these goals in mind, now we can set our family's financial goals and establish a realistic family budget.

The best way to reduce the amount of money you spend each month is to divide your spending into separate components and then identify ways to reduce spending in each area.

Notice the sample family budget on the following page in Figure 5. It outlines each spending category and also sets upper and lower targets to help you evaluate your situation.

Figure 6 provides a form for you to list your financial goals. For more information on how to complete your financial goals, see Chapter 9, "Eliminating Waste."

Figure 5
FAMILY BUDGET

INCOME PER MONTH	PAYMENTS PER MONTH
Salary _____	1. Tithe (10%) _____
Rent _____	2. Personal Savings (20%)_____
Other _____	A. Short-term _____
Other _____	B. Long-term _____
Other _____	3. Debt Repayment (0-10%)
Total Income	Major Loan _____
(less) Taxes _____	Credit Card _____
Net Income _____	Installments _____
	Other _____
	4. Housing _____
Net Monthly Income	A. Payments _____
	B. Lawn _____
————————————	C. Maintenance _____
	D. Taxes & Insurance _____
Total Expenses	E. Telephone _____
	F. Electricity _____
————————————	G. Gas _____
	H. Water _____
Coverage	I. Garbage _____
	5. Food (5-10%)
————————————	A. Groceries _____
	B. Sundry Items _____
	C. Eating Out _____
	6. Auto (10-15%)
NOTE: HAVE SAVINGS DEDUCTED DIRECTLY FROM YOUR PAYCHECK (PAYROLL DEDUCTION) IF POSSIBLE.	A. Payments _____
	B. Gasoline _____
	C. Maintenance _____
	7. Insurance (3-5%)
	A. Auto _____
	B. Health _____
	C. Life _____
	D. Other _____
	8. Entertainment/Recreation (3-5%) ____
	9. Clothing (3-5%) _____
	10. Medical (4-5%)
	A. Dentist _____
If you spend less than you earn, you will always have a surplus.	B. Doctor _____
	C. Other _____
	11. Miscellaneous (3-5%)
	A. Gifts _____
	B. Vacation _____
	C. Education _____
	D. Allowances _____
	E. Other _____

Figure 6
THIS YEAR'S FINANCIAL GOALS

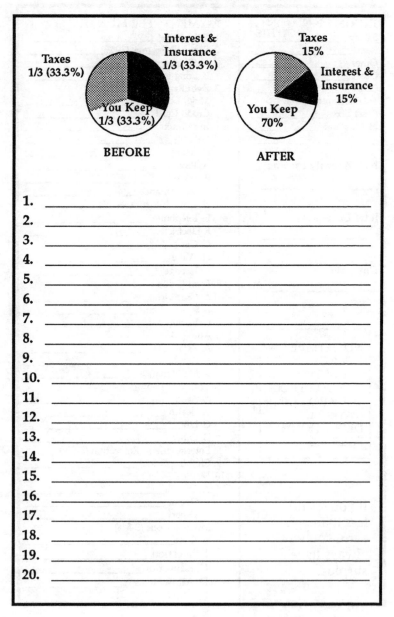

1. _____
2. _____
3. _____
4. _____
5. _____
6. _____
7. _____
8. _____
9. _____
10. _____
11. _____
12. _____
13. _____
14. _____
15. _____
16. _____
17. _____
18. _____
19. _____
20. _____

Figure 6, Continued

THINGS TO DO THIS MONTH	THINGS TO DO TODAY
1. _____	1. _____
2. _____	2. _____
3. _____	3. _____
4. _____	4. _____
5. _____	5. _____

CONCLUSION

Planning ahead is essential to being a good steward and developing a surplus to fund the preaching of the Gospel.

If you spend less than you earn, you will always have a surplus or savings account. A key to your financial future is to discipline yourself to set aside a portion of your income each month on a consistent basis and cut your expenses so that if something unforeseen should happen or God moves on your heart to do something for His kingdom, you won't be restrained from giving by your financial circumstances.

Satan has misled many Christians into thinking it is unspiritual to have a savings account or money set aside for emergencies or investments. They feel it shows an overall lack of trust in God's provision. As we have seen in this chapter, this is completely contrary to Scripture. As an investment banker working with individual and institutional finances, I have seen this attitude cause havoc in families and the nation as a whole.

One principle clearly established in the Bible is the principle of planning ahead and setting aside a portion of your income when times are good for future needs. The Bible states in Luke 16 and Proverbs 21:20 that a person is wise who stores up in time of plenty and prepares for the winter slack. So be wise and plan ahead!

4

DEALING WITH DEBT
BREAKING THE SPIRIT OF BONDAGE

The rich ruleth over the poor, and the borrower is servant to the lender.

Proverbs 22:7

Love not the world, neither the things that are in the world. If any man love the world, the love of the Father is not in him. For all that is in the world, the lust of the flesh, and the lust of the eyes, and the pride of life, is not of the Father, but is of the world.

I John 2:15-16

Larry and Connie were pastors of a church with a large membership. "I think the worst mistake I made was when we decided to borrow money from the church members," Larry said.

I listened as the story unfolded. Larry had been in the ministry twenty years. Over the past fifteen, his church had experienced tremendous growth. During this time, he also started a successful Christian school in addition to his church ministry. Because of the growth, he wanted to expand his facilities.

"It seemed so simple, I thought, since we were taking in enough money to meet the notes when we were in a smaller building," Larry continued. "I decided to move forward with the planned construction of a larger church. To secure financing, we had to use the school and ministry's other property as collateral for the land and new facilities.

"Everything seemed to be going okay until a major plant closed in our area. The income of the church dropped tremendously. If we didn't come up with some way of paying the monthly note, the lenders were threatening to foreclose. We would lose both the church and school, as well as the money some of the members lent the church," Larry said.

Another principle governing success in God's financial system is the principle of surety or the improper use of debt. A person will never be able to become totally free financially if he or she doesn't understand the principle of surety as it relates to debt.

This is a tragic case, but such situations occur more times than you can imagine for individuals and businesses alike. When a person incurs debt to finance a new purchase and has to risk existing assets to secure the loan, this is called surety, and God has much to say about such activities in the Bible.

This chapter is designed to help you understand how debt works and the power that debt has over our lives. For the average family, one-third of their income goes toward principal and interest payments.

HOW DEBT TAKES CONTROL

The seed of financial problems is normally planted early in an individual's life as a child watches and observes parents. Many children are never taught the basics of how to handle money. Consequently, as they grow up they feel they should immediately have everything that their parents took a lifetime to acquire.

ACTION STEP:
NEVER PUT FURNITURE, CLOTHES
OR PERSONAL ITEMS ON A
CREDIT CARD OR CHARGE ACCOUNT

The average young family starts off by purchasing an automobile, furniture and clothing on credit. This starts a debt pattern that usually sets the tone for the rest of their lives. Once this cycle is set into motion, it is not easily broken. By the time the first items are paid, the couple usually finds something else that they feel is needed. Gradually their income becomes consumed by interest and monthly payments, and they have no surplus.

ACTION STEP:
PAY OFF YOUR CREDIT CARDS IN FULL EACH MONTH
OR CUT THEM UP AND RETURN THEM

Once the credit card extends easier access to credit with higher ceilings and lower minimum payments, the cycle is almost complete. The grip of debt is tightened, often ending in destruction of personal integrity, bankruptcy and even a breakup of the family.

WHAT IS DEBT?

The basic definition of debt is this: An individual or corporation makes a commitment to purchase a product or service and agrees to pay the obligation in the future. This obligation normally takes the form of principal and interest payments.

However, debt is much more than monthly payments. Debt is a spirit. And when it gets out of control, it can render you useless to the kingdom of God. It becomes your master. It can weaken the basic foundation of the average family. Debt comes as a result of greed and a lack of self control, and it is usually accompanied by improper personal financial planning or no planning at all.

ACTION STEP:
REALIZE THAT GOD WANTS YOU OUT OF DEBT!
AVOID SURETY — NEVER RISK WHAT GOD HAS
ALREADY GIVEN BY BETTING ON FUTURE INCOME

Debt is a thief. It robs us of our time and money.

Debt causes worry, anxiety and thus conflict with family members and friends. Debt destroys our Christian witness. It prevents us from being a blessing to God and others. For most of us, when we become bogged down in debt our attention turns inward to personal problems. We spend most of our time trying to earn money just to meet our obligations. There is no money left to help someone who might be in need. We are held in bondage. In too many cases, we can be captured by the spirit of debt for a whole lifetime without even realizing it.

WHAT DOES GOD'S WORD SAY ABOUT DEBT?

The Bible is quite clear about the subject of debt. Debt falls under the general guidelines of borrowing, lending and surety outlined in the Bible. Borrowing money is not a sin, but God's Word has a lot to say about debt; i.e., making promises and obligating our future time and resources.

ACTION STEP:
NEVER MAKE A COMMITMENT
OF YOUR TIME OR MONEY
WITHOUT EXAMINING THE CONSEQUENCES

It is critical to exercise patience to break the spirit of debt. All Christians should be very careful about making commitments that bind us to do something in the future that might conflict with what God has planned in our lives.

In examining what the Bible says about debt, we must note that in addition to the general categories of borrowing and lending, anytime we note the terms usury, trust, vows, co-signing, striking hands and surety, the Bible is referring to debt in one form or another.

What does the Word of God have to say about debt? The borrower puts himself or herself in servitude to debt:

The rich ruleth over the poor, and the borrower is servant [slave] to the lender.

Proverbs 22:7

This is certainly true: A person who's heavily involved in debt is a slave to his or her debts in both time and money. Also pointed out in this scripture is that debt will ultimately keep that individual poor, if not used properly. By its very nature, it requires the transfer of wealth from the borrower to the lender, from one individual to another.

Paul also writes:

Owe no man any thing, but to love one another.

Romans 13:8

Ye are bought with a price; be not ye the servants of men.

I Corinthians 7:23

The main thing, however, is that God doesn't want us so bogged down in the world economic system that we can't do His will in the earth with our lives.

Love not the world, neither the things that are in the world. If any man love the world, the love of the Father is not in him. For all that is in the world, the lust of the flesh, and the lust of the eyes, and the pride of life, is not of the Father, but is of the world.

I John 2:15-16

HOW TO DOUBLE THE MONEY YOU KEEP

Ye have sown much, and bring in little; ye eat, but ye have not enough; ye drink, but ye are not filled with drink; ye clothe you, but there is none warm; and he that earneth wages earneth wages to put it into a bag with holes.

Haggai 1:6-7

Most families can more than double their disposable income by eliminating principal and interest payments. As pointed out earlier in the pie charts, for the average family, each dollar spent can be divided into three categories: One third for taxes, one third for interest and insurance and one third for bills, usually for principal payments. (See Figure 2, Chapter 3).

By establishing a budget and planning ahead, you can substantially increase your disposable income. (See Figure 3, Chapter 3). The following chapters will show you how to reduce interest, insurance and tax payments so you can have more disposable income to build a surplus.

Figure 7

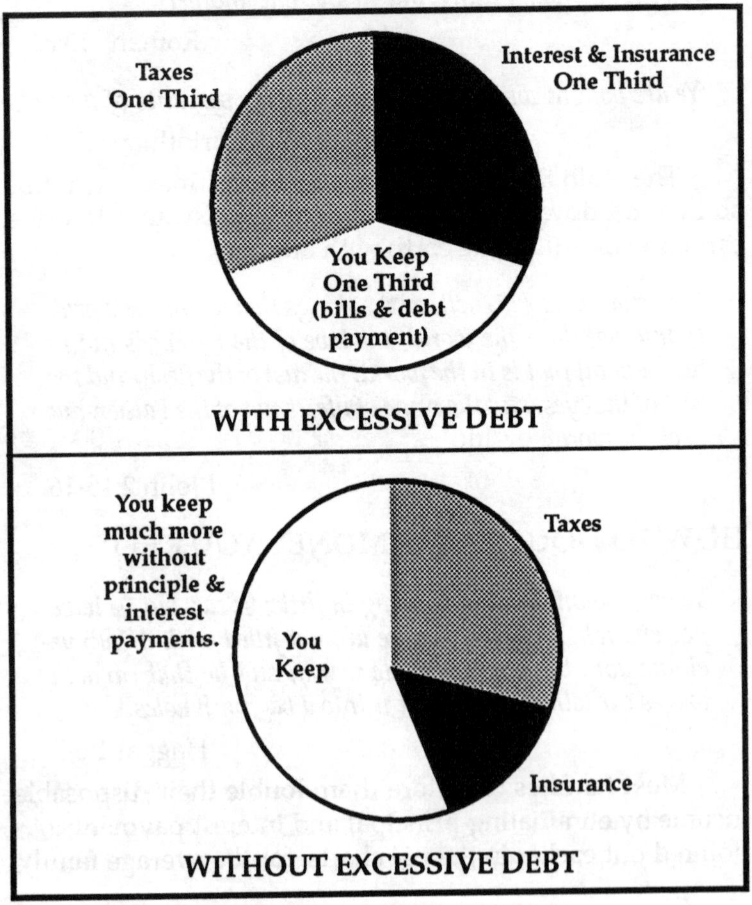

Taxes
One Third

Interest & Insurance
One Third

You Keep
One Third
(bills & debt
payment)

WITH EXCESSIVE DEBT

You keep
much more
without
principle &
interest
payments.

Taxes

You
Keep

Insurance

WITHOUT EXCESSIVE DEBT

Figure 7 shows the increase in disposable income the average family can keep without debt principal and interest payments.

ACTION STEP:
ESTABLISH A DEBT REDUCTION PLAN
IMMEDIATELY TO REDUCE
PRINCIPAL AND INTEREST PAYMENTS

To take control of your personal finances, you must take control of the three areas shown in the pie charts. Perhaps the most important element in these charts is debt.

As pointed out in Figure 7, you can substantially increase your disposable income by simply eliminating principal and interest payments (debt).

HOW TO BREAK THE POWER OF DEBT

By using the debt reduction plan in this chapter, the typical family can be completely debt free and be earning interest income to build wealth in five years or less.

But before we go farther, let's take a closer look at the greatest impact that debt is having on our lives. Debt has become a serious problem in our country over the past 20 years. It can be divided into three major categories:

1. National debt

2. Corporate debt

3. Personal debt

To understand the magnitude of the debt problem, let's examine these three aspects.

NATIONAL DEBT: The federal government is a major debtor. Because of overspending, our country has moved from being the number-one creditor nation to the world's largest debtor nation in a matter of a few years. Our budget deficit is approaching five trillion dollars. It is projected that the interest on our national debt will cost more than the entire military budget in the near future, approaching 20 percent of total national expenditures. And the country is rapidly approaching the point where it will not be able to collect enough taxes to pay the interest on the national debt. This, of course, would bankrupt our economy.

CORPORATE DEBT: The 1980s were known as the decade of mergers and acquisitions. Many of our bedrock corporations, in order to grow and expand their influence, purchased smaller subsidiaries using junk bonds. As a result, many of our best known and strongest corporations have been burdened with excessive debt.

PERSONAL DEBT: Personal debt takes the form of home, automobile, furniture, department store and, of course, credit card purchases. In examining personal debt, we notice the same trend in government and corporations. Individual borrowing also has increased at an alarming rate. The world system has completely indoctrinated Christians and non-Christians alike into thinking it is impossible to live in our society without being head over heels in debt. Because of the Wall Street/Madison Avenue mentality, many individuals find themselves making purchases that far exceed their ability to repay. As a result, many families are only one paycheck away from total financial disaster.

IN THE OLD TESTAMENT, DEBT IS A CURSE

In the Old Testament, debt is considered a curse. In examining the principle of borrowing and lending, the Scripture states:

And it shall come to pass, if thou shalt hearken diligently unto the voice of the Lord thy God, to observe and to do all His commandments which I command thee this day, that the Lord thy God will set thee on high above all nations of the earth: And all these blessings shall come on thee, and overtake thee, if thou shalt hearken unto the voice of the

Lord thy God...thou shalt lend unto many nations, and thou shalt not borrow.

Deuteronomy 28:1-2,12

But it shall come to pass, if thou wilt not hearken unto the voice of the Lord thy God, to observe to do all His commandments and His statutes which I command thee this day; that all these curses shall come upon thee, and overtake thee...The stranger that is within thee shall get up above thee very high; and thou shalt come down very low. He shall lend to thee, and thou shalt not lend to him: he shall be the head, and thou shalt be the tail.

Deuteronomy 28:15, 43-44

This has certainly come to pass in our country and in the lives of many families. They are the tail and not the head because they did not listen to God's Word regarding debt.

Another important aspect of debt is that it always makes a presumption on the future. It presumes first of all that you will have the money to pay the obligation. Second, it presumes that you will be alive to meet the debt. The Scripture states, however:

Go to now, ye that say, Today or tomorrow we will go into such a city, and continue there a year, and buy and sell, and get gain: Whereas ye know not what shall be on the morrow. For what is your life? It is even a vapour, that appeareth for a little time, and then vanisheth away. For that ye ought to say, If the Lord will, we shall live, and do this, or that.

James 4:13-15

FINANCIAL FREEDOM GOD'S WAY

A good steward realizes that $100,000 invested at 20% interest will produce the same income as working all year for $20,000. A good steward understands how money works and plans ahead to develop a surplus.

According to Deuteronomy 28:44, God expects you to be the head and not the tail. Under the borrowing and lending principle, the Bible indicates that you should be the lender, not the borrower. This implies that you should have a surplus in order to be in a position to lend and give to others. As a Christian, this is part of your economic destiny.

ACTION STEP:
SET A GOAL TO HAVE A SURPLUS ACCOUNT

Notice the picture the following scriptures paint:

He that hath pity upon the poor lendeth unto the Lord; and that which he hath given will He pay him again.

Proverbs 19:17

But love ye your enemies, and do good, and lend, hoping for nothing again; and your reward shall be great, and ye shall be the children of the Highest: for He is kind unto the unthankful and to the evil.

Luke 6:35

Give to him that asketh thee, and from him that would borrow of thee turn not thou away.

Matthew 5:42

He is ever merciful, and lendeth; and his seed is blessed.

Psalm 37:26

A good man sheweth favour, and lendeth: he will guide his affairs with discretion.

Psalm 112:5

God wants us to have enough of a surplus to lend and give to others.

LET INTEREST WORK
FOR YOU, NOT YOU FOR IT

Is it okay for Christians to receive interest on their money? Regarding interest, the Bible states that there are certain times when interest can be charged, and there are other times when interest should not be charged:

If thou lend money to any of my people that is poor by thee, thou shalt not be to him as an usurer, neither shalt thou lay upon him usury.

Exodus 22:25

And if thy brother be waxen poor, and fallen in decay with thee; then thou shalt relieve him: yea, though he be a stranger, or a sojourner; that he may live with thee. Take thou no usury of him, or increase: but fear thy God; that thy brother may live with thee.

Leviticus 25: 35-36

Thou shalt not lend upon usury to thy brother; usury of money, usury of victuals, usury of any thing that is lent upon usury.

Deuteronomy 23:19

ACTION STEP:
USE THE INTEREST ON DEBT
TO BENEFIT THE KINGDOM OF GOD

There are certain cases, however, in which it's okay to charge interest. As a matter of fact, God implemented the principle of interest in the Bible. It's normally called usury:

Unto a stranger thou mayest lend upon usury; but unto thy brother thou shalt not lend upon usury: that the Lord thy God may bless thee in all that thou settest thine hand to in the land whither thou goest to possess it.

Deuteronomy 23:20

In this scripture, we have two categories of lending — to a stranger and to a brother. Brother means a member of that individual's household or a fellow Jew. These verses tell us it is okay to charge interest. A Christian should be a wise manager and skillful investor, acting as a wise steward over all the resources with which he or she has been entrusted.

ACTION STEP:
ALWAYS PAY ALL DEBTS
YOU HAVE CREATED

A Christian also should be a wise steward of anything that he or she might borrow from another Christian or non-Christian. Regarding the repayment of debt, the Scripture states that if a man borrows anything from his neighbor and the property is damaged or destroyed, the borrower shall make full restitution:

The wicked borroweth, and payeth not again: but the righteous sheweth mercy, and giveth.

Psalm 37:21

WHAT ABOUT SURETY?

The Bible states that we should avoid putting ourselves in a position of surety. The dictionary definition of surety is a person who agrees to be legally responsible for the debt, default or conduct of another. And the biblical definition of surety is: Making a debt or commitment without having a sure way to repay the debt (collateral worth more than the debt), whether it's for yourself or someone else. Notice what the Scripture says about surety.

Be not thou one of them that strike hands, or of them that are sureties for debts.

Proverbs 22:26

> ### ACTION STEP:
> ### LEARN WHAT IT MEANS TO BE
> ### IN A SURETY POSITION: THEN
> ### DON'T ALLOW YOURSELF TO BE TRAPPED

A man void of understanding striketh hands, and becometh surety in the presence of his friend.

Proverbs 17:18

He that is surety for a stranger shall smart [suffer] for it: and he that hateth suretiship is sure.

Proverbs 11:15

My son, if thou be surety for thy friend, if thou hast stricken thy hand with a stranger, Thou art snared with the words of thy mouth, thou art taken with the words of thy mouth. Do this now, my son, and deliver thyself, when thou art come into the hand of thy friend; go, humble thyself, and make sure thy friend. Give not sleep to thine eyes, nor slumber to thine eyelids. Deliver thyself as a roe from the hand of the hunter, and as a bird from the hand of the fowler.

Proverbs 6:1-5

Surety is security against loss, damage or failure to do something. A good example of surety is when you purchase a car (the collateral) and the debt for which you obligated yourself is more than the market value of your car. If you bought the automobile for $10,000 with a $2,000 down payment, and then for some reason you could not meet the monthly payment for the balance of $8,000 and the car (the collateral) was picked up and the debt canceled, then you would not be in a surety position. The automobile would be collateral sufficient to satisfy the debt. You would have a sure way to pay.

If the automobile were worth enough to cover the debt, you would not have put yourself in a surety position. On the other hand, however, if they repossessed the automobile and you still owed the balance of the debt, you would have put yourself in a surety position.

If, for some reason, you can't pay a bill and the lender repossesses the collateral, and you have to tap other resources to pay the balance of the debt, you are in a surety position.

The same could be true for real estate transactions. Suppose you bought a duplex apartment, appraised at $100,000, for which the bank agreed to lend you $80,000. With the building as collateral for the debt, you would not have put yourself in a surety position.

If something should happen and you couldn't pay the monthly note and the bank repossessed the building, you would lose your $20,000 down payment; but you would not be obligated to pay the balance. Then you would not be in a surety position. The building would serve as collateral for itself. There would be a sure way to repay the loan.

DECEPTIVE SURETY

Many families are in a surety position and don't realize it. In a real estate market that was increasing in value over the last 40 years, you could always sell your home for a price that was higher than what you paid. In recent years, however, with real estate prices decreasing, many people have found themselves in a home that is actually worth less on the market than the balance they owe. They are in a surety position.

ACTION STEP:
EXAMINE YOUR HOME, ASSETS
AND BUSINESS TO SEE
IF YOU ARE IN A SURETY POSITION

The best way to avoid a surety position on your home, car or business is with a sufficient down payment. Where there is a sufficiently high amount of equity involved, surety is usually avoided. If the lending institution agrees to receive the property as full payment for the debt in case something should go wrong, you have a sure way to repay the loan. You are not in a surety position.

With credit cards, you are extremely vulnerable to surety. You should pay your credit card debt in full at the end of each month. If you don't have the money to pay in full, you should not use the card because you would be breaking the surety principle.

Business surety is an area of big problems in the United States. As an investment banker, I have had the opportunity to see many business transactions involving a great amount of debt. Debt is a tool like any other financial instrument, but if it is not used properly, it can cause great problems for a business. Many businesspeople take calculated risks with a portion of their income as investment to receive a future return on their money. A certain amount of risk is involved in any business.

However, there are other businesspersons who are constantly betting their entire future and business on "one roll of the dice," that one major business deal. In essence, what they are doing is going into surety, using resources that they have already accumulated as collateral to borrow on the future. What happens if a particular project should fail? The businessperson would lose the money he or she has already accumulated, plus the current business, not to mention his or her reputation. Such a person would have to start over, often losing a life savings and disrupting the lives of employees of the business in the process.

ACTION STEP:
NEVER PUT ALL YOUR EGGS
IN ONE BASKET

As Christians, we should never put ourselves in a surety position. We should never risk our entire business or savings on any one project. As good stewards, according to Luke 14:28, we should examine the outcome and count the cost before the commitment is made. Furthermore, even in the best of times, we should never "put all our eggs in one basket."

We should make sure that we can follow through on a commitment. But before even making a commitment, we should always examine its consequences and make sure it follows biblical guidelines.

ACTION STEP:
ALWAYS AVOID HASTY DECISIONS
WHERE DEBT OR INVESTMENTS ARE INVOLVED

COMMITMENTS, COVENANTS & CONTRACTS ARE SERIOUS TO GOD

The biggest problem we have in the area of debt and surety is that of commitment. In Joshua 9:3-20, Joshua made a commitment to live with kings. Although he was deceived because the kings lied to him, Joshua had to live up to the commitments that he had made. He had to follow through, even though his commitments caused him great difficulties later.

The Bible states that we should count the cost before we build a house:

For which of you, intending to build a tower, sitteth not down first, and counteth the cost, whether he have sufficient to finish it?

Luke 14:28

This is certainly true as it relates to our personal finances. We should never make a commitment beyond our ability to pay. We should examine all areas of the obligation prior to making a long-term commitment of time or money.

SURETY: WHEN YOUR LIABILITIES ARE MORE THAN YOUR ASSETS

A condition of surety that is often misunderstood is when an individual's liabilities are greater than his assets. (A person's debt is greater than the market value of what he or she owns.) This is a result of someone overspending his or her salary. If an individual is earning $2,000 per month but is spending $2,200 per month, he or she is already in a surety position or rapidly approaching it. Because the average family does not keep records, they often are unaware that they are spending more money than they take in by using credit cards. These debts usually accumulate over a period of time and ultimately cause serious financial problems.

One way to determine if you are in an overall surety position is to total the value of all your assets. If your total debt owed on assets exceeds current market value, you are already in a surety position. If you were to liquidate your assets, you would not have a way to pay the balance of your debt. In essence, you have to count on future earnings to pay your obligation.

HOW TO GET OUT IF YOU ARE IN OVER YOUR HEAD

If you are trapped by the debt cycle, how do you get out? It takes discipline. Now that you know what to look for, you can focus on the solution. There are five practical steps that you can take to break the power of debt in your life and to get out if you are in over your head.

ACTION STEP:
PRAY AND ASK GOD TO BREAK
THE POWER OF DEBT IN YOUR LIFE

Remember that the borrower is in bondage to debt. According to Proverbs 22:7, the borrower is servant to the lender. God's desire is for us to be debt-free, to have a surplus and to be able to lend instead of borrow.

For you to get your financial house in order and live above your financial circumstances, you must make a firm commitment to break the power of debt in your life.

ACTION STEP:
STOP BUYING THINGS ON CREDIT

This will be the most difficult step to take after you make a firm commitment. Put all credit cards and charge accounts on hold. To have victory over debt, you must stop buying things on credit. Stop all deficit spending. Instead of using credit cards, use cash. If you don't have the money, do without. You should never spend more money than you take in.

ACTION STEP:
START A DEBT REDUCTION PLAN IMMEDIATELY

ACTION STEP:
START A SAVINGS PROGRAM

If you spend less than you make, you will always have a surplus. You should set a goal to live on 70 percent of your income. (See Chapter 3 on planning.) With a surplus account, you will be able to set aside a portion of your income for emergencies, to purchase things you really need and to start an investment account for your family. This will be discussed further in the chapter, "Saving and Investing." The main point we are making here is to start where you are with your existing income and set aside something from every paycheck — even if it is only $5 to $10 per month. Set aside something.

ACTION STEP:
START GIVING ACCORDING TO THE SCRIPTURE
AND BELIEVE GOD FOR AN INCREASE

As you get debt under control, begin to immediately reach out to those around you — family, relatives, friends, neighbors and co-workers. Once your debt is under control and you are living above financial circumstances, reach out and help someone else learn how to get their personal finances under control. Here are some guidelines:

1. Take a portion of all the money that you save on interest and give it to your local church (church you are attending).

2. Set a goal to give more than 10% (tithe) of your income to the Lord's work.

3. Set up a reserve account specifically for giving to the poor and those who are in need.

4. Identify those ministries that have a proven record for missionary outreach and winning souls. Give liberally to these ministries. Remember, your money is an extension of you, and it can go places and work on your behalf.

START A DEBT REDUCTION
PLAN IMMEDIATELY

Start implementing a debt reduction plan immediately. To get out of the bondage of debt and live a debt-free life, you must make a serious commitment, then prepare a written plan. The basic elements of this plan are listed below:

1. Set a goal to get out of debt and be determined to see it through. Once you stop deficit spending, you have taken a major step to have victory over debt.

2. Determine how much money you owe. Get a total of your bills, and don't leave anything out. You need to know where you are financially. (A) Use the debt listed on the budget sheet in Chapter 3 to determine how much you owe. (B) Fill in the budget sheet provided for you in Chapter 3 to get an accurate account of your monthly expenses.

3. Prioritize bills from the smallest to the largest. This is very important. Determine which bill has the smallest number of remaining payments.

4. Once you have identified the smallest bill, focus your attention on paying it first. You can give your action plan a boost by going through your home and identifying things you don't really need. Sell them and apply the cash to that first bill.

5. After bill Number 1 is paid, take the money that you were paying on bill Number 1 and apply it to bill Number 2. Then start paying on bill Number 2 until it is paid in full. After bill Number 2 is paid off, focus on bill Number 3 until it is completely paid. Repeat this process until all your debts are paid.

CONCLUSION

In an effort to become free from financial bondage, we must remember that there are principles outlined in the Bible that will bring us through any financial difficulty.

There are five we have outlined so far in this book that will work by simply acting on the principles themselves. These biblical principles are as follows:

1. Remember that God owns it all. As stewards, we should follow His instruction.

2. Write down your financial goals. Start where you are and plan ahead to get maximum benefit from every dollar.

3. Establish a budget and live within your means. Set a goal to live on 70% of your income.

4. Set something aside from each paycheck.

5. Avoid surety (long-term and uncollateralized debt).

These principles are simple. For many of us, however, they may require drastic changes in our current lifestyles.

PRACTICAL APPLICATION

If you find yourself over your head in debt and want to start applying these principles to your life immediately, remember the following points:

1. Put God first. Plant a seed to God out of your first fruits.

2. Pay yourself second. Whatever you give to God, you want to be in a position to set aside an equal amount for yourself (minimum). You must always have a surplus account (cash reserve), or you will be right back where you started at the onset of the first emergency.

3. Reduce bills and outgoing expenses.

4. Use your budget and live on a cash basis. If you don't have the cash, don't buy it.

5. Avoid any new debts.

5

GIVING AND RECEIVING
OPENING THE WINDOWS OF HEAVEN

Honour the Lord with thy substance, and with the firstfruits of all thine increase: So shall thy barns be filled with plenty, and thy presses shall burst out with new wine.

Proverbs 3:9-10

Give, and it shall be given unto you; good measure, pressed down, and shaken together, and running over, shall men give into your bosom. For with the same measure that ye mete withal it shall be measured to you again.

Luke 6:38

I recall how my father managed his money when I was growing up. He simply brought his paycheck home to my mother, and she took care of all the bills. But I remember one time when he cashed his check and went out on the town with some friends. By the time he got home, nearly all his money was gone.

Needless to say, my mother didn't think much of this approach to giving. But that's the way my father looked at money. If it had been up to him, he would have given it away. He never met a stranger, and he never turned anybody down who had a need or asked to borrow money. He loved to help anyone who was in a financial bind or had some kind of business venture. As far as I can remember, he never knew he was following biblical principles, but he had a giving heart.

As the oldest of ten children, I agreed with my mother. I never understood why my dad gave so much away. I wasn't aware of it at the time, but we were considered a poor family. Yet my father was always giving things away. I didn't realize until many years later that my father had learned to tap into the principle of giving and receiving. As a result, he always had something to give, and it seemed he always had opportunities coming his way. What was it about my father that allowed him to always have something to give?

As I look back, I see the results of my father's giving. He raised ten children and put four through college; and now in his later years, he owns property in several locations — all paid for. This is not a bad financial situation for a person who never finished high school.

Many individuals go through life without learning about sowing and reaping. However, this principle of giving and receiving will work for anyone who uses it. It will work for the Christian and non-Christian alike.

As Christians, we are supposed to have an impact for the kingdom of God. We are supposed to be God's agents for good on the earth. But all too often we spend all our time to earn money just to pay bills. We don't have anything left to give.

One of the tragedies of our welfare system is that it restricts people from giving. It forces people to become takers, not givers, and then to turn totally inward. Welfare recipients become stagnant. The best way to get people off welfare is to teach them how to become valuable to someone else. They need to learn how to give of themselves first.

GIVING AND RECEIVING

The purpose of this chapter is to deal with some areas of giving that are overlooked in many Christian circles. There are biblical guidelines for giving and receiving that every Christian should understand. Giving is God's way for us to tap into His supernatural blessings.

As we look around, we see this principle at work in the world. Think about the philanthropist who puts money into a foundation to be given away, even though the motivation may have been to save on taxes. The more this person gives, the more blessings come his or her way. Or consider the businessman who puts money into a new business venture with the expectation of receiving a return. They call this "seed money."

The law of sowing and reaping will work for whoever operates it. Giving is one of the most powerful principles outlined in the Bible as it relates to our personal finances. But perhaps it is also one of the most misunderstood. Every Christian should understand the benefit of giving to God with the right attitude:

> *But this I say, He which soweth sparingly shall reap also sparingly; and he which soweth bountifully shall reap also bountifully...And God is able to make all grace abound toward you; that ye, always having all sufficiency in all things, may abound [give] to every good work: As it is written, He that dispersed abroad; he hath given to the poor: his righteousness remaineth for ever.*
>
> II Corinthians 9:6, 8-9

Many Christians realize that they are supposed to give, but they are having problems in their personal finances because they don't understand the giving and receiving cycle.

GIVING AND RECEIVING — TWO SIDES OF THE SAME COIN

To fully understand giving, we must realize that giving and receiving are two sides of the same coin. To be able to give from one side, you must have already received into the other side.

Of course, you can pledge a gift. However, according to the following scripture, you can only give after you have received.

For if there be first a willing mind, it is accepted according to that a man hath, not according to that he hath not.

II Corinthians 8:12

You can only give after you have received. According to the Scripture, God gives seed to the sower so that a person will have something to give.

Now he that ministereth seed to the sower both minister bread for your food, and multiply your seed sown, and increase the fruits of your righteousness.

II Corinthians 9:10

God always initiates the process.

For God so loved the world, that He gave His only begotten Son, that whosoever believeth in Him should not perish, but have everlasting life.

John 3:16

Notice that God so loved us that He gave first. God gives to us, then He allows us the opportunity to give back out of what we have.

Upon the first day of the week let every one of you lay by him in store, as God hath prospered him.

I Corinthians 16:2

RIGHT IN THE HEAD BUT WRONG IN THE HEART

I was counseling a Christian businessman in a city in which we were conducting one of our small-group study courses. The businessman explained his business had been successful; however, now he was having problems. He stated when he started to trust God, everything started to go wrong. "You can't run a business according to biblical guidelines and be successful; the two just don't mix," he said.

After examining his situation, we found the problems started after an evangelical meeting in which the minister made the statement, "You can't outgive God." Therefore, the businessman went to his cash register and took all the cash receipts and put them into the offering. He then began to "trust God to meet 100 percent of his needs."

In essence, you can't "outgive God," but you must also use wisdom and common sense. There are other principles in the Bible that govern our finances besides just giving, and this businessman had just broken most of them. One of these is honesty and integrity. (See Chapter 6.) All the money in the register did not belong to the businessman to give! A portion of every dollar he took in had already been promised to others for the general operating expenses of the business (suppliers, employees' salaries, utilities, etc.)

The problem was he had gotten just a part of the overall picture. He was only a trustee for the money he had mismanaged. The same is true with our individual finances. As stewards, if we don't set aside a portion of our income, we will be at the mercy of every emergency and problem that the devil sends our way. Once we promise to pay our utilities, credit cards and other living expenses, we have made a commitment, and the money no longer belongs to us. We do not have the spiritual authority to give it away.

But if we are obedient to God's Word, then we are in a position for God to supernaturally meet our needs.

There are some times when God will lead us to make sacrificial gifts, as He did the widow who gave her last mite or the woman who shared her last meal with the prophet Elijah. Notice God never asked them to break any biblical principle that He had given in the past.

Ignorance is no excuse with God. He wants our hearts and our actions to line up with His Word.

GIVING IS A FORM OF
THANKSGIVING TO GOD

Giving is a form of expressing thanksgiving to God for what He has already given you. Once you have given, you have completed the giving and receiving cycle. You have been blessed; now you have the opportunity to be a blessing to others.

Receiving is as simple as giving. You receive first, then give out of what you receive. Many Christians are waiting for their ship to come in: "When I earn $100,000 a year, I will give more to the Gospel. When God blesses me with more money, I will give to the poor." What are you doing with what you have now?

With most people, the future never comes. If you have a problem giving $100, you will have more difficulty giving $1,000.

The cycle is set. You start where you are. By giving out of what you have, God will bless you with more to give in the future. Now God knows you can be trusted.

GIVING IS A COMMITMENT
YOU MAKE IN ADVANCE

I believe in the last days God will raise up individuals in the local church who can be trusted to give large sums of money to finance the Gospel. We know that God wants us to be in a position to give. Many Christians go through their entire lives with a desire to give, but they simply don't have the money. They have problems just meeting their needs. How can they give to their local church or to the poor?

What is the problem? The answer is simple. Being in the position to give does not just happen; you must plan ahead today to be in a position to give in the future!

It is not a feeling or emotional outburst that happens suddenly. You must set a purpose in your heart (in advance) to be a giver.

In the earlier chapter on planning and preparation, we suggested that you set aside a specific portion of your income up front. The remaining 30% should be distributed among short-term and long-term savings and giving. One of your primary concerns should be giving. The purpose of this book is not to dictate the amount a person should give, but that God should be at the top of your list.

God must be included in your planning. The tithe (10%) is the standard measuring stick for many Christians. Yet, I believe that 10% is only a beginning point for your giving and that your giving should be led by the Holy Spirit. As a steward, remember God owns it all. The more you can direct toward His kingdom, the better.

By using the biblical principles outlined in this book, you may be in a position to give 90% and live on 10%. To ever fulfill the desire God has put in your heart to be a giver, you must make a commitment to do it in advance.

GIVING TO GET

Another area of difficulty for many Christians is that of giving to receive something in return. Many Christians give money specifically to get more money from God. They believe that if they give a certain amount of money to certain causes, God is obligated to do something on their behalf just because they gave.

Let us look at this area from a biblical perspective. It is not just indiscriminate giving that gets God's attention. You must give in faith according to biblical guidelines.

The main reason some receive more seed than others is because they have learned how to plug into the sowing and reaping principle. They know that when you plant a crop of soybeans, you will receive soybeans. The more you plant, the more you receive. The better the ground and the better the cultivation, the greater the crop.

You should give in faith, expecting to receive a return based on God's Word:

But this I say, he which soweth sparingly shall reap also sparingly; and he which soweth bountifully shall reap also bountifully. Every man according as he purposeth in his heart, so let him give; not grudgingly, or of necessity: For God loveth a cheerful giver.

II Corinthians 9:6-7

These verses clearly point out that giving will cause material increase, but giving should also be a condition of the heart.

And God is able to make all grace abound toward you; that ye, always having all sufficiency in all things, may abound to every good work.

II Corinthians 9:8

This passage goes on to say that God will give seed to the sower.

As it is written, He hath dispersed abroad; he hath given to the poor: his righteousness remaineth for ever. Now he that ministereth seed to the sower both minister bread for your food, and multiply your seed sown, and increase the fruits of your righteousness.

II Corinthians 9:9-10

Nevertheless, we know that everyone does not have seed to sow. The question is "Who has the sower's heart?" God will provide seed to those who are willing to sow.

THE SOWER'S HEART

Who has the sower's heart? If you were a businessman and were looking for someone to farm your land, which would you choose: a person who is a professional farmer or a person who believes he can be a good farmer? Who would more likely produce the best crop — the person who has been doing it for years with a proven track record or the person who says that he knows how to farm, but has no experience? The answer is obvious. The person with the proven track record would more likely produce the best crop. The experience he received from planting last year's crop gives him the experience to produce a better crop this year.

The same is true with our personal finances. The reason why some Christians don't have more seeds to plant is because they don't have a giving heart. They don't have experience in giving and a proven track record. They have not prepared themselves to be in a position to give.

We will discuss giving as a step of faith to receiving God's supernatural increase in more detail in Chapter 11.

GIVING OURSELVES FIRST

When we speak of giving, we must first give ourselves to God:

Present your bodies a living sacrifice, holy and acceptable unto God, which is your reasonable service.

Romans 12:1

The greatest gift to mankind was when God gave His only begotten Son Jesus Christ to the world. He gave because of His great love for us that is beyond anything we could ever comprehend. Because of the precious gift that God has given to us through His Son Jesus Christ, we should also want to give to Him in return.

Our giving should come out of a personal relationship with Christ — a relationship of seeking His guidance and direction for our lives and having a daily walk with Him. We have a great responsibility as Christians to be sensitive to His Holy Spirit and give as we are led.

Giving is an attitude of the heart. We give cheerfully because we love the Lord and want to see His will done on the earth.

When you give, you should give in faith, with an expectancy that God will multiply your seed as He said in His Word.

73

We should make sure we understand that whenever God makes a promise in His Word, we are responsible to do our part to receive the promise. Based on this system, we know that God gives material blessings, but we must realize that there are other biblical principles that also have an impact on our personal finances.

Just because we give does not automatically obligate God to intervene in our personal finances. There are other principles outlined in the Bible that also have an impact on the outcome of our financial circumstances. If you give on one hand but break other biblical principles governing your finances on the other hand, then your financial house will still be out of order.

HOW TO LAY UP TREASURES IN HEAVEN

God has a special concern for the poor and needy:

Hearken, my beloved brethren, Hath not God chosen the poor of this world rich in faith, and heirs of the kingdom which He hath promised to them that love Him?

James 2:5

He that hath mercy on the poor, happy is he.

Proverbs 14:21

He that hath pity upon the poor lendeth unto the Lord; and that which he hath given will He pay him again.

Proverbs 19:17

In these scriptures, we see that when we give to the poor, we are lending to the Lord. The poor are not able to repay us; so God repays us. He cares about the needs of the poor, who are always with us.

For ye have the poor always with you.

Matthew 26:11

Yet the Bible goes on to say that it is our responsibility as Christians to help meet the needs of those who are less fortunate than we are. We are God's vessels to use to bless others in need.

ACTION STEP:
SET A GOAL OF GIVING TO THE POOR

It is very important to notice the impact that giving to the poor has for laying a foundation in heaven. Notice the following scripture, in which Jesus told a rich young ruler:

One thing thou lackest: go thy way, sell whatsoever thou hast, and give to the poor, and thou shalt have treasure in heaven:...take up the cross, and follow me.

Mark 10:21

There is treasure in heaven when we give to the poor.

Charge them that are rich in this world, that they be not highminded, nor trust in uncertain riches, but in the living God, who giveth us richly all things to enjoy; That they do good, that they be rich in good works, ready to distribute, willing to communicate; Laying up in store for themselves a good foundation against the time to come, that they may lay hold on eternal life.

I Timothy 6:17-19

As it is written, He hath dispersed abroad; he hath given to the poor: his righteousness remaineth for ever.

II Corinthians 9:9

Lay not up for yourselves treasures upon earth, where moth and rust doth corrupt, and where thieves break through and steal: But lay up for yourselves treasures in heaven, where neither moth nor rust doth corrupt, and where thieves do not break through nor steal.

Matthew 6:19-20

Sell that ye have, and give alms; provide yourselves bags which wax not old, a treasure in the heavens that faileth not, where no thief approacheth, neither moth corrupteth.

Luke 12:33

GIVING WITH THE RIGHT ATTITUDE

There are a variety of conflicting attitudes regarding giving. When I was growing up, I went to church every Sunday with my grandparents. Since my grandfather was the preacher, I had the opportunity to observe firsthand what happened with the offering. Although my grandfather was a committed Christian, he never preached a sermon on giving. His focus was always on winning souls to Jesus. The offering was just another necessary part of the service, so the attitude of most was, "Let's get it over with as quickly as possible."

I observed the reaction of the congregation while the offering plate passed by. I noticed that several members were always late. They arrived just after the offering was over. Then there were the faithful, who would always put in a dollar and who usually would give a coin to their children so they could give also. Next were those who looked as if it were an imposition for them to pass the offering plate and put in nothing. Still there were others who felt it was an obligation to put something in the plate.

As I look back, I see that my childhood experiences governed how I gave to the church as I became an adult. Because I never had been given a biblical foundation, I formed my attitudes by what I saw others do.

As I talk to Christians today all over the country, I find many of them grew up pretty much the same as I did. Some grew up in churches but never understood the importance of giving and receiving principles. Many Christians don't want to give because they don't understand what the Scriptures really say regarding giving.

Once a Christian who genuinely loves the Lord learns what the Bible says about giving and receiving, his or her attitude about giving changes.

Listed in the next section are some of the more common questions received during the Stewardship in Action — Small Group Study workshops.

PRACTICAL APPLICATION: QUESTIONS AND ANSWERS ON GIVING

Q. What about sacrificial giving? Is it always right to give sacrificially?

A. Yes, sacrificial giving is very much a part of God's giving plan. It is for emergency situations and is discussed throughout the Bible. But, it is not always the best way to give and not for every situation. God never intended for us to live from emergency to emergency.

Q. If you give to the poor, what part of your budget would the money come from?

A. The money would come from the surplus, not the tithes and obligations you owe other people. It should be set aside for this purpose.

Q. Is God obligated to perform a miracle in your finances just because you give or have a need? Why or why not?

A. No. Faith must be operating. You must be obedient to do what God's Word says. If you do your part, God will do His part.

Q. Can you plant a seed of something other than money and receive financial blessing? If so, explain.

A. Yes, give whatever you have: time, love, friendship, abilities, talents, etc. Consider the passage in I Kings 17:11-16, about the woman with a handful of meal and a little oil. She gave her last cake to the prophet and received a great blessing that lasted until the drought was over. She gave (planted) the meal and oil, which was all she had, and received a harvest through her obedience. (The same is true of Joseph and Daniel.)

Q. What is the main purpose of giving? Is it for your benefit or God's benefit? Explain.

A. Our benefit. God does not need our money. God uses giving as a means to bless us and to establish His covenant in the earth. The money never leaves the earth; only the things you do with the money go toward your heavenly account.

Q. What is the principle of sowing and reaping that's involved when a businessman uses seed capital to start a new business? Describe.

A. He sows money into a business, and he reaps a harvest when the business becomes profitable.

Q. What about the principle of gleaning — how does it apply to seed time and harvest?

A. God provided a method in the Bible called gleaning, a means of giving to the poor out of the abundance God has given you. The guidelines for gleaning were presented in the Old Testament. An example of this can be found in the passage of Ruth 2:15-23. You will find that God makes special provisions for the poor throughout the Bible. There is always a blessing for taking care of the poor. (Gleaning was not a part of the tithe.)

Q. Do you feel that God wants us to live from one financial crisis to another? Is God obligated to perform a miracle just because we are in a financial crisis?

A. No. If you stand on God's Word, trust in Him and are obedient to what He says, He will deliver you. God operates according to His Word. If you obey His Word, God has obligated Himself to perform according to His Word.

Q. What about gimmicks used by preachers to make you give?

A. That is not an acceptable reason to give to God. You should be led by God's Spirit when giving to a ministry.

Q. What if you give and you find out that the minister didn't do what he said he would with the money?

A. If you gave in faith and had the right attitude as a steward, God will honor it. Remember, you are not giving to the minister, but unto God. However, if you find a ministry that is not honest, you should make every dollar count for the kingdom of God and give your money accordingly.

Q. Should you give to bums and derelicts who ask for money?

A. It depends. If you feel led of God, do it. If you do not feel led of God, it is best not to give. You may want to give as an opportunity to witness to those in need.

6

HONESTY AND INTEGRITY
THE FOUNDATION FOR ALL GOD'S BLESSINGS

The just man walketh in his integrity: his children are blessed after him.

Proverbs 20:7

A good name is rather to be chosen than great riches, and loving favour rather than silver and gold.

Proverbs 22:1

This was an essay question that a freshman college student had to answer for an English composition class: "What is one of the most memorable events you recall from your childhood?" Her answer was a touching recollection, which described the underlying strength of the character of her family.

She described an event that had stuck with her through the years. Her mother went to a restaurant's drive-through window. She gave the cashier a $20 bill and took the change in her hand. With the kids in the car, she drove away without counting the money. She had almost gotten home when she noticed that the attendant had given her more money than she should have. It appeared that she had given her a $10 bill instead of $1. The mother turned the car around and drove halfway across town to return the change to the restaurant. She told the attendant that she had given her too much change. "It is nice to meet an honest person these days," the grateful attendant said.

The young lady noticed that her mother never really said anything to her children, but that day they learned what real honesty was. Honesty is not a matter of money, but a condition of the heart. It is doing the right thing, even when it seems not to be in your best interest.

HONESTY AND INTEGRITY BRING BLESSINGS AND WEALTH FROM GOD

Honesty and integrity will make you successful in God's financial system. Honesty and integrity open the door for God to come into your financial circumstances.

Honesty and integrity are the foundation for receiving God's supernatural increase. All blessings from God, including financial blessings, come as a result of an honest heart. Honesty and integrity will definitely have an impact on your finances. Notice the importance that honesty will have in our lives:

• Wealth will be in the house of the honest and upright person: *In the house of the righteous is much treasure: but in the revenues of the wicked is trouble* (Proverbs 15:6).

• Your children will be blessed: *The just man walketh in his integrity: his children are blessed after him* (Proverbs 20:7).

• Even if you make mistakes, God will lift you up: *For a just man falleth seven times, and riseth up again: but the wicked shall fall into mischief* (Proverbs 24:16).

• An honest person is valuable to others: *The tongue of the just is as choice silver: the heart of the wicked is little worth.* (Proverbs 10:20).

• Honesty will keep you out of trouble: *The wicked is snared by the transgression of his lips: but the just shall come out of trouble* (Proverbs 12:13).

• A good name and honest reputation are much more valuable than great riches: *A good name is rather to be chosen than great riches, and loving favour rather than silver and gold* (Proverbs 22:1).

• A truthful person is a delight to God: *Lying lips are abomination to the Lord: but they that deal truly are his delight* (Proverbs 12:22).

• *Ye shall not steal, neither deal falsely, neither lie one to another* (Leviticus 19:11).

• If you are honest, God will guide you: *The integrity of the upright shall guide them: but the perverseness of transgressors shall destroy them* (Proverbs 11:3).

• God will not withhold any good thing from the honest and upright: *For the Lord is a sun and shield: the Lord will give grace and glory: no good thing will He withhold from them that walk uprightly* (Psalm 84:11).

• Honesty and integrity will preserve you: *Let integrity and uprightness preserve me; for I wait on Thee* (Psalm 25:21).

• God will be merciful and bless those who walk in integrity: *But as for me (David), I will walk in mine integrity: redeem me, and be merciful unto me* (Psalm 26:11).

• *Better is the poor that walketh in his integrity, than he that is perverse in his lips, and is a fool* (Proverbs 19:1).

• God will be intimate with the honest person: *For the froward is abomination to the Lord: but His secret is with the righteous* (Proverbs 3:32).

• An honest person will be established forever: *The lip of truth shall be established for ever: but a lying tongue is but for a moment* (Proverbs 12:19).

• An honest man will not take bribes and will keep trouble out of his house: *He that is greedy of gain troubleth his own house; but he that hateth gifts [bribes] shall live* (Proverbs 15:27).

• An honest person will not lie to become rich: *The getting of treasures by a lying tongue is a vanity tossed to and fro of them that seek death* (Proverbs 21:6)

God is looking for individuals who have honesty and integrity of heart to trust with the true riches.

CAN YOU BE TRUSTED?

A class I taught was discussing the day's homework assignments when Janet began to speak. She explained that her son worked as a local supermarket cashier. He came home one day and told her about something that happened to him. He had gone to the bank to cash his check, and when he returned to work he discovered the cashier had put $100 too much in his envelope by accident. His co-workers told him that since it was the cashier's mistake, he should keep the money.

However, he went to his supervisor and told him what had happened and asked if he would let him off work for a half hour so he could return the money.

As their instructor, I pointed out to the group, "Janet's story is a good example of honesty and integrity."

Janet quickly added, "That's not the whole story." She went on to explain that about four months later, her son's cash register came up short of money. Her son indicated that he had done nothing wrong, but he could not explain how the money had disappeared from his register.

Normally the cashier would have been immediately fired, but his supervisor was not convinced that he took the money because of the earlier incident with the $100. It was learned that someone had used Janet's son and set a trap without his knowing anything. Another individual had been using the number to his register to get access to it without anyone knowing. The main reason the son didn't get fired was because his manager did not believe that a thief would have returned $100 to a bank when the bank had made a mistake. This story illustrates the value of having a good name (reputation).

According to the Bible, it is true that God has promised to bless us financially. But it is also true that God allows financial blessings to be taken away from those who don't have integrity of heart or those who don't know how to properly handle the money with which they have been entrusted.

Take therefore the talent [money] from him, and give it unto him which hath ten talents. For unto every one that hath shall be given, and he shall have abundance: but from him that hath not shall be taken away even that which he hath.

Matthew 25:28-29

For riches certainly make themselves wings; they fly away as an eagle toward heaven.

Proverbs 23:5

Wealth gotten by vanity shall be diminished: but he that gathereth by labour shall increase.

Proverbs 13:11

HOW GOOD IS YOUR WORD?

Can you really be trusted to keep your word? Do your words say one thing and your actions say something else? Are you honest in everything that you do? Christians must walk in honesty and integrity — honesty before God and honesty before man. Living in our day, in this society, we are all confronted every day on matters of honesty and integrity. When we go to the cafeteria, are we tempted to try to avoid paying for items that we have received? At the grocery store, when we go through the checkout line, if we receive more money in return than we should, do we return it? On our taxes, do we overstate certain deductions? Concerning insurance, do we add more to our claims than should really be there to receive greater benefits than we deserve?

ACTION STEP:
WALK IN TOTAL HONESTY WITH GOD AND MAN

ACTION STEP:
HAVE CONFIDENCE THAT GOD
WILL PERFORM HIS PROMISES

If we believe, in fact, that God's Word is truth, we must act on His Word as if it's true. This is the basic definition of faith. God promised in His Word that He'll take care of us, that He'll meet our needs if we accept the promises He has given us. Then we can walk in certainty and believe that God will perform the promises that He's made. Lying and being dishonest indicates we do not have complete trust in God's Word to provide what He says He will provide for us in our lives:

> *He that walketh in his uprightness feareth the Lord, but he that is perverse in his ways despiseth Him.*

Proverbs 14:2

Being honest with God is having confidence in His Word and that His Word is true.

ACTION STEP:
ALWAYS BE HONEST
WITH FRIENDS AND CO-WORKERS

Most activities of dishonesty are caused by one person who cares more about his or her own desires than the desires of another person. Most of the problems that we have in today's society come as a result of someone wanting to take advantage of property that someone else owns.

Because of advertising and our materialistic society, we've been taught to covet things that belong to others. We are "programmed" to want a bigger home and a larger car. From television and other secular entertainment, we are taught to covet even our neighbors' wives and husbands. The basic perception is to look out for Number 1. This is the system that operates in the world. But God has another system, and it operates on a totally different set of principles and guidelines:

Thou shalt love thy neighbour as thyself.

Romans 13:9

God wants you to be honest in your business and work affairs. Even the smallest dishonesty displeases God and is a sin. In examining the stewardship principle in the Bible, we read:

Whosoever is dishonest with very little will also be dishonest with very much.

Luke 16:10 (NIV)

Do you feel you have to tell a little white lie to protect yourself and protect your property? In work and business, are you honest with your employer? Are you honest with your employees? As a worker, God wants you to be an example to the people who work around you. Do you provide an honest day's work for an honest day's pay?

Do you carry yourself in a way that projects honesty in everything you do?

ACTION STEP:
ALWAYS PROVIDE AN HONEST DAY'S WORK
FOR AN HONEST DAY'S PAY

Do you get to work on time? Do you take a few extra minutes for your coffee breaks? Do you take things home from work that don't belong to you? God's requirement is that we be honest first before Him and then before our neighbors and the people around us.

ACTION STEP:
ALWAYS BE HONEST WITH YOUR EMPLOYEES;
LOOK OUT FOR THEIR INTERESTS

> ## ACTION STEP:
> ### AVOID PERSONAL AND BUSINESS
> ### ASSOCIATION WITH DISHONEST PEOPLE

OTHER TELLTALE SIGNS
OF A DISHONEST HEART

Because of the decrease in society's standards, many people are dishonest without every realizing it, even Christians. Can you be trusted with money? Do you have a bad credit report? Do you pay your bills on time? How we conduct ourselves will have an impact on people around us. Likewise, we are influenced by people with whom we work and associate.

> ## ACTION STEP:
> ### MAINTAIN A GOOD REPUTATION —
> ### PAY YOUR BILLS ON TIME

A good name and reputation should be maintained at all times. Keep your word; pay your bills on time and don't make commitments that you can't keep.

A good name is rather to be chosen than great riches, and loving favour rather than silver and gold.

Proverbs 22:1

If a man vow a vow [makes a promise] unto the Lord, or swear an oath to bind his soul with a bond [commit himself]; he shall not break his word, he shall do according to all that proceedeth out of his mouth.

Numbers 30:2

> ## ACTION STEP:
> ### NEVER VOLUNTARILY FILE BANKRUPTCY
> ### FROM YOUR DEBT

Bankruptcy is not an option for Christians. Certainly a Christian can get into a difficult situation regarding debt. But a Christian should not intentionally go in and purchase things with the thought that he or she can get out of paying for them by filing bankruptcy.

ACTION STEP:
ALWAYS MAINTAIN A GOOD CREDIT REPORT

How is your credit report? Always maintain a good credit report. Check your credit file and see if it has accurate information. Many times the credit reporting agency has outdated or inaccurate information. As a good steward, a child of God must be beyond reproach as he or she conducts business affairs before the unsaved world. Everything we do is under scrutiny and is a testimony to someone, whether that person realizes it or not. This is especially true in how we pay our bills and handle personal obligations.

ACTION STEP:
CHECK YOUR CREDIT REPORT ANNUALLY
TO MAKE SURE IT IS ACCURATE

As good stewards, we must keep our word. Joshua made a promise to the Canaan tribe. Even though he was deceived, he had to keep his promise. (Joshua 9.)

ACTION STEP:
ALWAYS KEEP YOUR WORD;
DO NOT MAKE PROMISES YOU CANNOT KEEP

There was a price that had to be paid simply because Joshua made a promise, even though he did not have all of the facts. The Scripture states in Deuteronomy that it is better not to make a vow than to make a vow and not keep it. We must keep our vows, our commitments and promises that we've made.

CONCLUSION

We must walk honestly before God and man. Our name is worth more than money.

God is looking for people He can trust to be coworkers with Him in establishing His covenant in the earth. Your name is a combination of the words you speak and the actions you take.

We must remember as Christians, every one of our actions is a testimony to someone around us. What we say, what we do and how we conduct our business are all being closely watched by the unsaved to see if what we claim about Christ is working in our lives.

Our lives should be a living testimony to the unsaved and Christians alike at work, at home and in the eyes of the general public — that God's way of doing business is not only different from the world's way of doing business, but God's way is better.

There's no better way to judge a person's character than to watch how he or she handles money during hard times. God wants us to be a good witness and bear a good testimony in the earth. He wants our words to be consistent with our actions. Our name should be synonymous with character and integrity.

If we are not diligent with unrighteous money, we won't be diligent with the true riches. When we make a vow, we must keep it. If we promise to pay a bill on a certain date, we must pay it on that date, even if it means we have to make a personal sacrifice to do it.

PRACTICAL APPLICATION

Read the following questions. If you are involved in any of these activities or other activities you feel would not be pleasing to God, ask God to forgive you. Then make a specific effort to correct these areas. Set personal goals to eliminate any of the items that you feel God is bringing to your attention.

Ask yourself the following questions on honesty and integrity:

1. Am I on time for appointments or am I constantly late?

2. Do I report all income on my taxes and all my expenses legitimately? Do I have bounced checks on my personal checking account?

3. Do I keep my promises to my children?

4. Do I provide an honest day's work for an honest day's pay?

5. Have I made a vow (pledge) to God (or man) but not kept it because I needed it more? Do I spend more money than I earn?

6. Do I care for others' property as well as I do my own; i.e., my employer's property and property that I borrow or use that belongs to someone else?

7. Do I have a habit of telling only partial truths or stretching the truth or telling little white lies?

8. Do I find myself avoiding friends and relatives because I owe them money?

9. Do I ever misappropriate office supplies, stamps, or anything else of my employer's?

10. If I am undercharged for a purchase in a checkout line, do I keep the money or report it?

11. When dealing with other people, do I look out for their interests as well as my own?

12. Do I have bad credit? Am I honest in meeting my obligations and keeping commitments that I've made?

13. When I sell a car, house or other property, do I tell the whole story; or do I keep something back that I should reveal to get a larger profit?

7

WORK AND DILIGENCE
RELEASING OPPORTUNITY IN YOUR LIFE

He becometh poor that dealeth with a slack hand: but the hand of the diligent maketh rich.

Proverbs 10:4

Be thou diligent to know the state of thy flocks, and look well to thy herds.

Proverbs 27:23

As I sat across the desk from Pat, a former Stewardship in Action — Small Group Study Course student, I heard her say, "My husband and I had something very interesting happen to us last week."

"Okay, what was that?" I asked.

"Mal just got an increase in pay at his job," Pat said, speaking of her husband.

"That's good news," I said. "Tell me what happened."

"Do you remember that at one of your workshops, you said we should try to make ourselves valuable to our employers?"

"Yes, I remember that."

"Well, Mal thought about that, and at work he noticed that the grass around the edge of the parking lot needed to be cut. He figured that because he didn't have a college degree, he would not be able to do some of the other things at the warehouse. So he took it upon himself to tackle this particular chore. Without being asked, he started to cut the grass and keep the lawn clean at no request for pay.

"This continued for awhile without special recognition for the job. Then last week one of the marketing employees moved on to another job. The owner of the business asked Mal if he would like to have the marketing job, which had the potential for much greater increases in pay. He also asked Mal if he would like to take over the maintenance contract on the building, which would be an additional $300 to $400 per month above the salary paid for the new job."

God rewards diligent work, and God will reward the work of your hands — if you do your work as unto God, not man.

And whatsoever ye do, do it heartily, as to the Lord, and not unto men; Knowing that of the Lord ye shall receive the reward of the inheritance: for ye serve the Lord Christ.
Colossians 3:23-24

Let him that stole steal no more: but rather let him labour, working with his hands the thing which is good, that he may have to give to him that needeth.
Ephesians 4:28

For even when we were with you, this we commanded you, that if any would not work, neither should he eat.
II Thessalonians 3:10

DILIGENCE AND HARD WORK BRING PROSPERITY WHILE LAZINESS BRINGS POVERTY

Another biblical principle that prepares us for God's supernatural increase is diligence and hard work. Work is the pathway out of poverty. Diligence and hard work will change your financial circumstances. If you work, you will be rewarded. Diligence and work go hand in hand.

All work is honorable. Work provides an income stream that gives you and God something with which to work. Notice the following scriptures:

But rather let him labour, working with his hands the thing which is good, that he might have to give to him that needeth.

Ephesians 4:8

He becometh poor that dealeth with a slack hand: but the hand of the diligent maketh rich.

Proverbs 10:4

The hand of the diligent shall bear rule: but the slothful shall be under tribute.

Proverbs 12:24

YOU MUST BE DILIGENT IN BUSINESS AFFAIRS

If you work, you can build wealth if you manage your money properly. Even if you are an average wage earner with a small income stream, God can supernaturally bless your income if you are obedient to follow His Word.

Seest thou a man diligent in his business? He shall stand before kings; he shall not stand before mean men.

Proverbs 22:29

Be thou diligent to know the state of thy flocks, and look well to thy herds. For riches are not for ever: and doth the crown endure to every generation?

Proverbs 27:23-24

If your household earns $25,000 a year, that is over one million dollars during a lifetime. Once you realize that it is God Who blesses you with money so that you can be a good steward, you must be diligent to manage it properly.

HOW TO PROSPER DURING
HARD ECONOMIC TIMES

Pat and Mal's story at the beginning of this chapter reminded me of another, concerning Sissy, with whom I worked at an investment company. She was in sales and marketing, but she wasn't doing well as a salesperson. At the time, her sales volume was low compared to the other sales staff. She was a diligent worker and tried hard to increase her sales but had no immediate success.

"We need someone to learn how to monitor the mutual fund activities," was a constant complaint from a number of more successful marketing people.

Since none of the other salespeople would take the responsibility because they felt it was a distraction, Sissy volunteered. "I will organize and file all the mutual fund material," Sissy said. She took on the added responsibility right away. After organizing the files, she began to keep track of each mutual fund's performance and took it upon herself to order each company's brochure to keep on file. Not only did she keep up with the major companies, she also assisted other salespersons in filing initial applications. She became known as the in-house mutual fund expert. Yet many of the salespeople ridiculed her for doing these extra services without additional pay.

Everything was going well in the investment business until the mini-crash of October 1987. Shortly thereafter many investment companies found themselves in trouble because of the change in the economy. The investment company for which Sissy worked had to cut back on staff by 50%. I saw Sissy at a restaurant sometime later and asked her how she was doing.

"Dwight, I'm doing great. You know, the company had to cut back, and they let half of the people go; but they kept me because they needed someone to handle mutual fund business. Also, my sales volume has picked up."

"Yes? That's great, but tell me about your sales increase," I answered.

"Well, after all the big-time salespeople dropped out of the business, the company gave me a chance to service some of the old accounts. Now my business has tripled what it used to be." God will always bless diligence and hard work!

HOW TO KEEP YOUR JOB WHILE EVERYBODY IS GETTING LAID OFF

ACTION STEP:
MAKE YOURSELF VALUABLE TO YOUR EMPLOYER —
LOOK FOR MORE WAYS TO HELP YOUR EMPLOYER
BECOME MORE SUCCESSFUL

What about following the examples of Mal and Sissy and making yourself valuable to your employer? Many things can be done:

And whosoever shall compel thee to go a mile, go with him twain.

Matthew 5:41

You can make yourself valuable by learning what your company is all about, then retraining yourself to assist your company to make more money or to help your employer save money in existing areas. Your responsibility as an employee is to make your supervisor look good, to make your organization look good.

Here are some ways to make yourself indispensable:

1. Be familiar with your company's overall business. Learn what it takes to make a profit and become valuable in the process.

2. Learn your job and the jobs of those around you. Assist others in their jobs.

3. Learn how to plant seeds. Take on responsibilities without having to be told to do so.

4. Be the first to help out when there is something extra that needs to be done.

5. Become dependable and trustworthy.

Because of your hard work and willingness to go the extra mile for your company, you will be rewarded not only by your boss, but God as well.

These principles are almost absent from the average work place. They have been replaced by this attitude: "I'll work if you pay me first. I'll do only the work that is required of me. I'll come in late and leave early. If I can get by with it, I'll do as little as possible on the job."

ACTION STEP:
DO YOUR WORK AS UNTO THE LORD
AND GOD WILL REWARD YOU

Many of us spend one third of our lives working, laying down a third of our lives to earn a paycheck. Therefore, it is important for Christians to balance our lives and learn how to submit work as a gift to God. God must have more than equal time. He must be in first place.

ACTION STEP:
DEDICATE YOUR WORK TO THE LORD
AND USE IT AS PART OF YOUR WORSHIP

HOW LONG SHOULD WE WORK?

God pointed out the general parameters for the amount of time we should spend working each week.

Six days thou shalt work, but on the seventh day thou shalt rest: in earing time and in harvest thou shalt rest.
                                                                    Exodus 34:21

We can see in our society that there is a wide variation to working schedules, but the most common is the eight-hour day, five-day week. The most important factor in answering the question of how much we should work that we should recognize as Christians is that we should work hard, but not overwork.

The current trend is to lean toward either of two extremes. The one extreme is not to work at all and depend on someone else or the government to furnish your needs. The other extreme is to become so involved in your work that you tend to neglect your family, health and God and overextend yourself.

A good way to keep work in balance is to remember your major priorities, as discussed earlier in this book: Your first priority is to God.

But seek ye first the kingdom of God, and His righteousness; and all these things shall be added unto you.
                                                                    Matthew 6:33

Your second priority is your family, and your third priority should be your profession. If you are neglecting God or your family by working, you are overworking. (See Ephesians 5:21-6:9.)

THE RESPONSIBILITY OF AN EMPLOYEE

An employee's responsibility is to be faithful to his or her employer. If you are an employee, remember that you have been hired to do a job so that your employer can make a profit. You must produce more than the expenses necessary to pay your salary to be productive to your employer.

And whatsoever ye do, do it heartily, as to the Lord, and not unto men; Knowing that of the Lord ye shall receive the reward of the inheritance: for ye serve the Lord Christ.

Colossians 3:23

If you take a job for a low salary, you should do your work just as if your employer were paying you double. If such is the case, God will move heaven and earth to reward you even if your employer or supervisor doesn't recognize your work, and you will be blessed. The blessing may come from a source other than your employer, but God will always find a way to bless a person who is diligent in work and works in faith as unto the Lord.

Many employees forget their responsibilities after they receive jobs. You should always do excellent work regardless of how you feel about your job or your employer. If you are doing your work as unto the Lord, your work will be of a quality second to none.

Servants, be obedient to them that are your masters according to the flesh, with fear and trembling, in singleness of your heart, as unto Christ; Not with eyeservice, as menpleasers; but as the servants of Christ, doing the will of God from the heart; With good will doing service, as to the Lord, and not to men: Knowing that whatsoever good thing any man doeth, the same shall he receive of the Lord, whether he be bond or free.

Ephesians 6:5-8

EMPLOYER'S RESPONSIBILITY

An employer is responsible for being honest and fair with his employees. An employer must look out for the interests of his or her employees as well as his or her own interests:

Masters, give unto your servants that which is just and equal; knowing that ye also have a Master in heaven.

Colossians 4:1

In the world's economy, the relationship expressed in the Scripture is often not the case. Many employers are not sensitive to the needs of their employees. Their intention is to push the employee as far as possible to do a maximum amount of work. This situation was the reason labor unions were formed — to protect the rights of the employee. If the biblical principle had been acknowledged by employers, it would never have been necessary for labor unions to develop.

Employers should always pay employees a fair and reasonable wage. Once an employee has performed his or her responsibilities, the worker should be paid on time:

Thou shalt not defraud thy neighbour, neither rob him: the wages of him that is hired shall not abide with thee all night until the morning.
Leviticus 19:13

FINISH WHAT YOU START

Whenever you take on a job, do it well. You should always make a habit of completing your work. Many of us make promises and take on responsibilities and never count the cost. Our lives become a series of unfinished projects. We are busy doing many things but leave many undone. Whenever God started something, He completed it and wants us to do the same. Remember, whenever you do a job, you should do it as if you are doing it for God and not man.

CONCLUSION

In conclusion, there are two things we should always remember. First, that God ordained work in the beginning. He created it for our benefit:

And the Lord God took the man, and put him into the garden of Eden to dress it and to keep it.
Genesis 2:15

This incident took place before the fall of man. Many individuals believe that work came as a result of Adam's sin and that work is part of the curse. But this scripture lets us know that God never intended for man to sit idly by and do nothing. He instituted work in the garden of Eden when man was created. The curse came later. (See Genesis 3:17-19.)

We work to earn money so that we can provide the essentials for our families to live. Paul states:

...that if any would not work, neither should he eat.
II Thessalonians 3:10

Another reason to work is to have enough money so that you can give to and extend a helping hand to others:

Let him that stole steal no more: but rather let him labour, working with his hands the thing which is good, that he may have to give to him that needeth.
Ephesians 4:28

Work will definitely have an impact on personal finances. It is an essential key to building a sound financial foundation.

Second, be diligent in everything to which you set your hands. Do your work as if you are working for the Lord Himself:

And whatsoever ye do, do it heartily, as to the Lord, and not unto men; Knowing that of the Lord ye shall receive the reward of the inheritance: for ye serve the Lord Christ.
Colossians 3:23-24

We should remember that God is our provider, not our employer.

PRACTICAL APPLICATION

In examining the practical side of work, remember when God gives you something, it will not put you in more bondage. There are five common mistakes related to work that should be avoided:

1. Never make your spouse work just to improve your lifestyle unless you are both in agreement and know you are fulfilling God's purpose in your lives.

2. God's wealth is a result of diligence and discipline. It is not dependent upon the amount of money you earn.

3. Make every dollar count. Look for ways to eliminate waste and buy things wholesale. Pay cash when it is in your favor.

4. Set a goal to spend less money than you earn so that you will have a surplus account.

5. Avoid quitting one job until you already have another or an alternative source of income lined up.

Remember that God is the provider of supernatural increase. If you are following biblical guidelines in your finances, you will be able to see an increase. Be patient, and God will always be faithful to His Word.

8

SAVINGS AND INVESTMENTS

CHANGING SURPLUS INTO ABUNDANCE

Steady plodding brings prosperity; hasty speculation brings poverty.

Proverbs 21:5 (TLB)

The wise man saves for the future, but the foolish man spends whatever he gets.

Proverbs 21:20 (TLB)

I was driving down the highway with my radio tuned to the news channel. Suddenly the national news headline was announced: "Custodial worker beats Wall Street." That immediately got my attention. I thought this was a strange opening for a national news update.

I listened anxiously for the follow-up story: "Custodial worker in Detroit leaves $700,000 to a Catholic girls' home." I wondered what was so spectacular about this incident. The custodial worker died, and the money was delivered to the girls' home. Another $380,000 also was found in a mutual fund account owned by the custodian.

The amazing part of this story was that no one could figure out how a person of 70 years of age with a humble job could have accumulated such a substantial sum of money. This was an unusual story. However, I was expecting the announcer to come back with a statement such as, "Custodial worker puts a few thousand dollars on stock option and wins a fortune." This would have been more spectacular.

I thought this was an interesting story, but why would it occupy a major part of the national newscast? Then it occurred to me that this was indeed a newsworthy story. The average American will never accumulate any real wealth because most spend everything they earn. They don't understand the value of compound interest. Many do not understand even the basic principles of saving and investing.

GENERAL OVERVIEW

A small surplus over time becomes abundance with the proper use of compound interest. This is a key principle that governs God's financial system and should be understood by every Christian. The next two chapters will concentrate on building wealth God's way by eliminating waste and properly redirecting resources you already have. They examine how money actually works, how to turn surplus into abundance, how to start where we are and how to use what we have as stewards over God's resources. We want to maximize the mileage out of every dollar God has entrusted to our care.

Many of the principles discussed in the following two chapters will be elementary to some, but life-changing and exciting to others. Keep in mind that the information given can function only as a guideline and is not intended to be used as a specific recommendation. Use it as a measuring stick for organizing your financial plan according to the goal that God has laid on your heart.

DEVELOPING YOUR SURPLUS

This subject has already been discussed in greater detail. (See Chapter 3.) If you spend less money than you take in, you will always have a surplus. Your first goal then, to becoming free from financial bondage, is to learn how to develop a surplus.

Satan understands that if he cannot keep you from developing a surplus, he cannot limit the amount of money you have to invest into the kingdom of God. You will have moved past just getting your personal needs met to being able to reach out to others.

As a steward of God's financial resources, God wants us to know that His abundance is already built into the system. However, you must use your faith and be obedient to God's Word in order to be a channel that God can use.

For unto every one that hath shall be given, and he shall have abundance: but from him that hath not shall be taken away even that which he hath.

Matthew 25:29

For ye know the grace of our Lord Jesus Christ, that, though He was rich, yet for your sakes He became poor, that ye through His poverty might be rich.

II Corinthians 8:9

But by an equality, that now at this time your abundance may be a supply for their want, that their abundance also may be a supply for your want: that there may be equality.

II Corinthians 8:14

After you develop a surplus, you must find a place to store it. Remember (from Chapter 3) God wants us to be good stewards over the whole dollar, not just part. We want to know what to do with the other 90% after we give 10% to God. Let's take another look at Figure 2, which we already introduced in Chapter 3, in order to get a better look at our outgoing budgetary dollar. (Go on to the next page.)

Figure 2

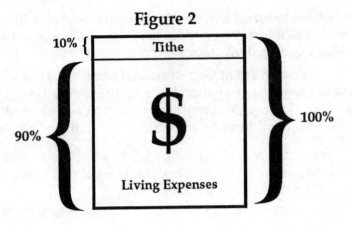

We then set a goal to live on 70% instead of spending everything we earn. With a minimum of 10% going to our local church, this leaves us with a surplus of 20%, as shown in Figure 4 below.

Figure 4

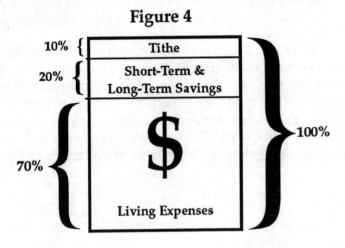

> *ACTION STEP:*
> *ORGANIZE YOUR SURPLUS ACCOUNT*
> *TO REFLECT THE CALL THAT GOD*
> *HAS PUT ON YOUR LIFE*

The 20% Figure 4 shows as surplus can be distributed between a short-term and long-term savings account.

To sort this surplus, there are 15 to 20 basic strategies the average Christian can use to eliminate waste and build wealth in God's economy. These strategies will be used as the basis for most of the action steps discussed in the next two chapters.

WHAT BANKS AND INVESTMENT COMPANIES DON'T TELL YOU ABOUT YOUR MONEY

This section provides answers to investment questions you may have always wanted to know but did not know who to ask.

You should take control of your personal financial affairs, never leaving them blindly to someone else to handle. The reason that banks and financial institutions are the most wealthy businesses in the country is because they look out for their interests first. The system is designed to work in their favor. Your interest comes as a secondary factor.

The information listed below presents insights you won't normally learn from your bankers or investment advisors:

1. You can be your own banker and invest your money at the same rate that the insurance companies and banks do (cutting out the middleman).

2. Fees and commissions will rob you of valuable investment resources and interest income.

3. Banks, insurance companies and investment bankers don't tell you how your money works; i.e., a small surplus over time becomes abundance with the proper use of compound interest.

4. If you spend less money than you earn, you will always have a surplus for investments.

5. Compound interest will make you wealthy if you allow it to work for you instead of them.

6. Time and consistency work in your favor. When you set a little bit aside each month, it will become a large amount over time.

7. You can start where you are, using what you already have, to begin your investment program by eliminating expensive fees and commissions.

HOW BANKS, INSURANCE COMPANIES AND INVESTMENT COMPANIES WORK

ACTION STEP:
AVOIDING PAYING UNNECESSARY
FEES AND COMMISSIONS

You should learn how insurance companies, investment companies and banks actually work. An insurance company makes money off of the premium you pay each month, and it profits from investing the surplus funds. Salespeople make a commission every time you buy a policy.

An investment company makes its money from commissions, fees and the interest it makes on money it has invested. Whenever you buy or sell an investment, you pay your broker a transaction fee and/or a commission. The broker makes money on each transaction regardless of the financial results you receive.

Banks operate on the same principle. They make money on the spread between what they pay you in interest on your savings and what they receive by investing your money. They also charge fees for transactions you make at the bank.

It is important for Christians to know that each of these institutions operate by encouraging you to bring your money to them so that they can invest it for you. In most cases, you can make the same investments for yourself and put the investment's income in your pocket instead of the institution's.

In most investment companies, the cards are stacked against the average investor. Most of the time the broker will be tempted to sell you the product which pays him or her the highest commission.

A no-load mutual fund means you do not pay commission up front when you open your investment account. By identifying no-load or low-load mutual funds, the average family can avoid paying excessive commissions and fees on their investment transactions.

USE COMPOUND INTEREST TO BUILD A MILLION-DOLLAR RETIREMENT ACCOUNT — STARTING FROM WHERE YOU ARE

Use payroll deduction to start an IRA (Individual Retirement Account). By investing a small amount of money over a period of time, even a modest investment can grow into a substantial retirement account. The key is time and consistency. One example is as follows:

If you invested $1,000 per year ($2.65 per day) at 9% interest at the age of 25, at the age of 65 (with compound interest), you would have $32,000. By using the "rule of 72," you can learn how many years it would take your money to double. In this particular example, by dividing 72 by 9%, you would find that it would take approximately 8 years for your money to double. (See Table 1.)

ACTION STEP:
LEARN HOW COMPOUND INTEREST WORKS

ACTION STEP:
USE THE RULE OF 72 TO DETERMINE
HOW LONG IT TAKES YOUR MONEY TO DOUBLE
AT A GIVEN INTEREST RATE

Table 1
9% INTEREST ($1,000)*

AGE	AMOUNT
25	$1,000
33	2,000
41	4,000
49	8,000
57	16,000
65	32,000

*(IF YOU START WITH A $1,000 INVESTMENT AT THE AGE OF 25 AND RECEIVED 9% INTEREST UNTIL AGE 65.)

In Table 1 you can see the effect of compound interest. If you had started with only a $1,000 investment at age 25, it would have grown to $32,000 by age 65.

To illustrate the point of what it means to be a wise and skillful investor, consider the following: If you receive $32,000 on a $1,000 investment at 9%, how much would you receive at retirement if the interest rate were 18% (about the average interest rate on major credit cards). Before you consult the next table, make a quick estimate of what you feel this amount would be at retirement. Now take a look at Table 2 to check your answer.

Table 2
18% INTEREST ($1,000)*

AGE	AMOUNT
25	$1,000
29	2,000
33	4,000
37	8,000
41	16,000
45	32,000
49	64,000
53	128,000
57	256,000
61	512,000
65	1,024,000

*(IF YOU START WITH A $1,000 INVESTMENT, USING COMPOUND INTEREST.)

STEADY PLODDING

Steady plodding brings prosperity; hasty speculation brings poverty.

Proverbs 21:5 (TLB)

The key to building a solid investment portfolio is to set aside a specific amount from each paycheck. Steady investing of small amounts produces the best results. For example, if a person puts $10.21 per month at age 25 into a mutual fund averaging 12% per year, he or she would have in excess of $100,000 at retirement. At 12% interest, this person could retire with $12,000 annual income without touching the principal.

If a person were to save $1 a day at 12% interest, he or she would accumulate more than $200,000 at retirement. This is less than the cost of one pack of cigarettes or a couple of trips to the soft drink machine. At 12% interest on the $200,000 principal, this person would earn approximately $24,000 per year in interest payments without touching the principal.

If a person saved $2.74 a day at 12.5 % interest starting at the age of 25, they would receive $1,148,000 at retirement. This is approximately $1,000 per year of total investment. At 12.5% interest on the principal, they would have an income of approximately $143,000 per year without touching the principal. If the investor increased the investment amount to $2,000 per year instead of $1,000, starting at age 25, the retirement principal would be $2,297,000. The monthly income on this amount would be approximately $24,000 per month or $288,000 per year without touching the principal.

Considering these examples, you can set your financial investment goals. By determining the amount of income you would like to receive upon retirement each month, you can identify the amount of money you need to set aside each month.

One of the best ways to build a sound investment account is to use an IRA (Individual Retirement Account). The government will allow you to set aside $2,000 a year tax free if you meet certain qualifications. Your base income would be taxed after the deduction for the $2,000. For example, if you earned $20,000 per year and you took a $2,000 IRA deduction, you would pay taxes only on $18,000. Therefore, you would be saving on taxes as well as getting interest on your investment.

By using this approach, you would receive a better return from your IRA investment than if you had invested after-tax dollars because you would receive interest on the full $2,000. If you had paid taxes on this amount at a 30% rate, you would only have $1,400 to invest instead of the entire $2,000.

The bottom line is, by being diligent and disciplining oneself to set aside a little of each paycheck and allowing compound interest to work on one's behalf, the average individual could easily accumulate a retirement account in excess of $1,000,000.

After reviewing these principles, it is clear how the low-paid custodian could accumulate enough to leave a substantial endowment for the charity of his choice upon his death.

ACTION STEP:
SPEND LESS MONEY THAN YOU EARN
AND YOU WILL ALWAYS HAVE A SURPLUS

Remember, if you spend less money than you earn, you will always have a surplus. The challenge, however, is to discipline yourself to live on 70% of your income. In the chapter on planning and preparation, this concept was introduced. By setting this 70% as a goal, you would be aiming at an objective that would automatically put you in control of your personal finances. If you learned to live on 70% of your income, you would always have a surplus to invest.

You must be faithful with what you have and start where you are. If you earn $12,000 per year, you must learn to live on less than $12,000 per year. If you do not learn to spend less than you earn, it won't make a difference if you earn $20,000, $50,000 or $100,000 per year. Your spending would simply rise as your income rose.

START NOW

According to the 1990 census, more than 75% of our population retire on less than $10,000 annually and more than 50% retire on less than $5,000 per year. I am sure that most of these people never intended to retire below the poverty level, but many made no preparation to avoid it.

You must start now and be diligent in order to use time and consistency in your favor. Table 3 shows that the sooner you get started, the better.

Table 3
START NOW

AGE	$1.00 PER DAY AT 12% INTEREST	COST TO WAIT
25	$296,516	-0-
26	$264,402	$32,114
30	$116,858	$179,658
COST TO WAIT FROM 25 TO 26 YEAR IS $32,114; UNTIL 30 YEARS, $179,658.		

SHORT-TERM SAVINGS

Your short-term savings is a holding account to cover your short-term goals. Some examples are as follows:

1. Extra offerings to the church, to give to the poor, extend a helping hand to others, or other things the Lord may lay on your heart. Your offerings are always above and beyond your tithe. They can never be taken from your living expenses, or it will throw your entire budget out of balance.

2. Your six months' emergency fund, which should cover six months' living expenses and other unexpected expenses.

3. Your savings and short-term purchases: appliances, auto, clothing, furniture, etc. Now that you are cutting back on debt and interest expenses, you are planning ahead for

purchases you need in the future. Impulse buying and debt are cut to a minimum.

4. To provide coverage for higher deductibles on your insurance: auto, home and health. By having a short-term savings account, you have substantially reduced overall living expenses. (See Chapter 3, "Planning and Preparation.")

ACTION STEP:
USE YOUR MONEY MARKET ACCOUNT TO STORE
YOUR SHORT- AND INTERMEDIATE-TERM SAVINGS

LONG-TERM SAVINGS

Since your long-term savings account is for long-term investments, this is your "not-to-touch money." The funds in this account should be used for the following items only:

• To provide a retirement income (IRA, Keogh, mutual funds, annuities, etc.).

• To create an estate (home, business, family support).

• To meet other long-term goals, such as college for yourself and children.

Since setting aside long-term savings is one of the most important steps the average family can take, there is always the temptation to put it off until later. And once you do set aside some funds, there is the temptation to use this money for some short-term emergency.

To illustrate the point, here is a personal story: Awhile ago, when both my wife and I were working, we made a decision to open an annuity account. We paid faithfully every month into this account for five years. Then we ran into one of our "regular" emergencies. After examining the circumstances, we decided that we would take the money out of our annuity account.

Because of my lack of understanding about financial planning, we made the same mistake that many families do.

We sacrificed our long-term savings in order to meet a short-term emergency. I found out later that this transaction was a costly mistake in a number of ways:

1. We lost our long-term investment. It would take a much larger monthly investment to get the same results the older we got.

2. We had paid a commission on the account, which reduced our initial investment.

3. We paid a penalty for early withdrawal.

4. Finally, we had to pay taxes on the money we received. (After five years, we actually had less money than we put in).

ACTION STEP:
USE YOUR NO-LOAD OR REAR-LOAD
MUTUAL FUND TO INVEST YOUR IRA
AND LONG-TERM INVESTMENTS

HOW TO EARN 20% ON YOUR LONG-TERM INVESTMENT ACCOUNT

There is no such thing as a risk-free investment. An investment that makes a 60% return in one year can lose 80% in the next year. It is impossible to pick the top or bottom of a rising market. You can only use interest rates as an indicator to establish trends. The idea of the money movement strategy is to earn an average of 20% per year, pay no commission and then pay minimum taxes on your earnings.

This objective can be accomplished by using your IRA account. You pay no commission up front when your IRA (individual retirement account) is invested in a no-load or rear-load mutual fund. Your account earns interest on your entire investment. There is, however, a small service charge by the money managers, whose cost is spread over the entire fund. You pay no taxes on your earnings until you withdraw your retirement fund at the age of 59 1/2.

Earning an average of 20% on your investment involves being in the right investment at the right time. As a rule, when interest rates are going down, you should have the majority of your investment in a bond mutual fund. When the current interest rate on the 30-year treasury bond is below 8 1/2%, you should have most of your investments in a family of no-load or rear-load stock mutual funds.

When the interest rate on the 30-year bond rises above 8 1/2%, you should move the majority of your investment funds to the money market account in the same no-load mutual fund. You should have your account set up for a telephone switching service so that these transactions can easily be accomplished. There are normally no commission charges for switching from stock, bonds or money market funds in the same family.

Figure 8
MONEY MOVEMENT STRATEGY

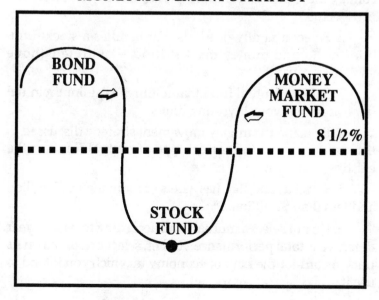

The chart on the previous page illustrates money movement strategy. You must be diligent in watching the change in long-term interest rates to receive the maximum benefits from this type of strategy. Otherwise, I suggest that you diversify in all three areas or get a broker whom you can trust to keep watch over your account if you don't have time.

HOW TO CHOOSE THE RIGHT NO-LOAD MUTUAL FUND

What is a no-load mutual fund? In simplest terms, "no-load" means no commission is charged to invest money into this particular mutual fund. This fact is important because your entire investment goes to work for you immediately.

Choosing the right mutual fund family is easy once you know what your objectives are. Following is a step-by-step guide.

1. Consult financial magazines. Each year they have a list of the top-performing mutual fund families. You can contact these mutual fund companies directly and ask for a prospectus.

2. Select a family of funds that handles a stock fund, bond fund and money market fund — with telephone switching capabilities.

3. Select a mutual fund that requires a minimum initial deposit within your investing limits.

4. By using the money movement strategy discussed in this section, select the correct type of mutual fund for the existing economy.

5. Select a fund that has assets of more than $25 million and less than $2 billion.

6. Do not select a mutual fund according to its five-year or ten-year total performance. Rather, select one based on its track record for the kind of economy in which you intend to use it.

Once you find a broker with whom you can work on the implementation of your long-term investment plan, he or she will normally have all the above information on file. Just ask your broker to send you a copy of the prospectus for the fund under consideration before you invest.

FIFTEEN BIGGEST INVESTMENT MISTAKES

There are a number of areas the average investor should avoid as a general rule. Listed below are the 15 most common ones.

1. Never use life insurance as an investment. Buy life insurance to provide death benefits.

2. Avoid individual stocks and bonds. Use a no-load or rear-load mutual fund for your investment needs. You pay no commission, and this approach takes a lot less time than researching individual stocks and bonds.

3. Never invest in bond funds when interest rates are rising.

4. Never buy investments over the phone from a broker you don't know.

5. Avoid buying stocks, bonds and mutual funds from brokerage houses without comparing prices. Normally you will pay very high commissions and unnecessary fees.

6. Never make an investment for tax savings alone.

7. Avoid borrowing money and using leverage funds to purchase stocks or bonds unless you have thoroughly researched the market and are an expert in that particular field.

8. Don't make investments based on hunches and tips from friends, relatives and anxious stock brokers without totally understanding the investment.

9. Avoid switching your investments from one account to another more than once or twice a year. Market timing is critical to receiving a 20% annual return, but unless you

121

have time to watch the market on a consistent basis, this process is too time consuming. Moreover, each transaction by a commissioned broker costs you money. (See discussion on receiving 20% on your investment.)

10. Avoid commissioned brokers unless they have demonstrated that they understand the biblical principles and guidelines set forth in the Bible and will assist you on a long-term basis to implement a sound broad-based financial plan.

11. Never waste money in time-sharing investment opportunities. Don't invest more than 5% to 10% of your investment portfolio in precious metals as inflation hedges.

12. Don't invest in get-rich-quick investments, such as volatile commodities.

13. Avoid options as a leverage or hedge on your investments.

14. Unless you have a lot of money to invest, avoid over-diversification. Choose the right type of mutual fund for the right economy.

15. Never buy expensive market-timing newsletters. No one knows when the market is going up or going down on a week-to-week or month-to-month basis unless that person is a money manager. Your main indicator should be the current long-term interest rate.

HOW TO CHOOSE A BROKER

1. Ask trusted friends who have dealt with no-load mutual funds in the past.

2. Identify an individual who understands no-load mutual funds and the value of term life insurance versus whole life and who will not try to pressure you to convert to a whole life policy six months down the road.

3. Try to locate a broker who understands the biblical principles for handling money and will be willing to use the 21 key strategies listed in Chapter 12 as a checklist to assist you in organizing your financial plan.

4. Become acquainted with the broker, but always compare his or her prices with other firms with the same product.

5. It is okay to pay a broker commission if the broker is willing to work with you on a consistent basis to keep your financial plan on track.

6. Take your time and make sure you understand every transaction. Don't be talked into purchases you don't understand.

7. Don't expect your broker to spend hours with you if you have a small account. Don't expect your broker to know when the stock market is going up or down. To conserve time, you should have your basic investment objectives clearly in mind before you call your broker.

ACTION STEP:
MAKE A HABIT OF PAYING
YOURSELF FIRST AFTER GOD

The ant is wise because he stores food in the summer to survive the winter. The summer of your life is when you are young and have time on your side. It is also the time when compound interest will begin to have the greatest impact. Unfortunately, however, this is the time we have the greatest appetite for consumption.

You should make a habit of saving. If necessary, you should force yourself to be thrifty. One way this can be done is a payroll deduction plan at work or through your credit union. By taking your savings off the top, you won't be tempted to spend your retirement.

ACTION STEP:
AVOID RISKY INVESTMENTS
AND GET-RICH-QUICK SCHEMES

Investments can cover a variety of areas. Never invest in any venture that you don't understand. The Bible says you should avoid speculative investments:

> *There is another serious problem I have seen everywhere, savings are put into risky investments that turn sour, and soon there is nothing left to pass on to one's son. The man who speculates is soon back to where he began with nothing. This, as I said, is a very serious problem, for all his hard work has been for nothing: he has been working for the wind. It is all swept away.*
>
> Ecclesiastes 5:13-16 (TLB)

The cause of most bad investments is greed, the thought of a quick buck, a large return on something you have not worked to earn. Nevertheless, one hears constant reports of people who lose their money trying to get a quick return.

ACTION STEP:
MAKE INVESTMENTS THAT WILL
PAY AN ETERNAL RETURN

YOUR BEST INVESTMENT

Your best investment is to invest in the kingdom of God.

> *Tell those who are rich not to be proud and not to trust in their money, which will soon be gone, but their pride and trust should be in the living God who always richly gives us all we need for our enjoyment. Tell them to use their money to do good. They should be rich in good works and should give happily to those in need, always being ready to share with others whatever God has given them. By doing this they will be storing up real treasure for themselves in heaven — it is the only safe investment for eternity! And*

they will be living a fruitful Christian life down here as well.

I Timothy 6:17-19 (TLB)

He gives generously to those in need. His deeds will never be forgotten. He shall have influence and honor.

Psalm 112:9 (TLB)

You invest in your heavenly account by sharing with others the resources with which God has blessed you while you are here on earth.

A faithful steward learns how money works. A faithful steward knows how to get a return on an investment. In Matthew 25, the two faithful stewards were rewarded because they had doubled their master's resources.

According to the Bible, it is wise to save for the future:

The wise man saves for the future, but the foolish man spends whatever he gets.

Proverbs 21:20 (TLB)

ACTION STEP:
ORGANIZE YOUR SURPLUS ACCOUNT

MONEY: THE ROOT OF ALL EVIL?

Money is neither good nor evil. However, a common myth passed down through religious tradition within the body of Christ states that money is the root of all evil. This is not what the Bible teaches.

For the love of money is the root of all evil.

I Timothy 6:10

The Scripture states clearly that it is the love of money that is the cause of all kinds of evil. Money is not evil in itself. This scripture has been grossly misquoted over the years. As a result, it has driven many individuals away from Christianity.

As a youngster living with my grandparents, I heard this scripture quoted incorrectly throughout the Christian community. My grandfather was a minister, and he lived a humble lifestyle. I noticed as the offering plate passed by that usually the largest bill in it was a dollar. Since the church was small, the collections were always limited. My grandparents and all the people whom I remember were poor. In spite of good upbringing by my Christian grandparents, I grew up thinking that to be a good Christian, you had to be poor.

This is not the attitude we should have as Christians. If money were the root of all evil, a good Christian logically would not want to be associated with money. The truth is that money will take the character of whoever has it. If you are a good Christian, your checkbook will reflect it. A good person will spend his or her money in a way that reflects character. Likewise an evil person's spending will reflect his or her character. It is not the money that is good or bad but what a person is willing to do to get it, or what one is willing to do with it after receiving it.

IT'S OKAY TO HAVE AN INVESTMENT ACCOUNT

It is scriptural to have a surplus. The Bible teaches this principle in both the Old Testament and New Testament. It is necessary to have a surplus to do what God asks you to do regarding giving and meeting the needs of the poor. How can you give to God's work if you are living from paycheck to paycheck and not setting anything aside?

You should at least have put my money on deposit with the bankers, so that when I returned I would have received it back with interest.

Matthew 25:27 (NIV)

If you spend less than you earn, you will automatically have a surplus. You will have to store your surplus money somewhere. Jesus states in Matthew 25 that you should at least put money into the bank to receive interest. Therefore, it is okay to have investments. It is also acceptable to receive interest on your investments.

PRACTICAL APPLICATION

To start to build wealth in God's financial system, you must act on the principles outlined in this chapter. Contact your investment advisor or financial planner and let that person know you want to implement the "21 Practical Steps to Build Wealth in God's Economy" outlined in Chapter 12. If you would like to have more information on how to implement the plan yourself, you should contact Urban Ministries for a catalog of tapes and support materials.

Those individuals who do not have a financial planner and would like individual assistance in organizing and implementing their financial plan should contact Nichols Financial Group. Financial counselors have been trained to assist you in organizing and implementing the 21-step plan based on the principles outlined in this book.

FOR MORE INFORMATION, CALL:

NICHOLS FINANCIAL GROUP

(313) 893-6842

DETROIT, MICHIGAN

9

ELIMINATING WASTE
CLOSING THE HOLE IN YOUR FINANCIAL BUCKET

*Ye have sown much, and bring in little; ye eat, but ye have
not enough; ye drink, but ye are not filled with drink; ye
clothe you, but there is none warm; and he that earneth
wages earneth wages to put it into a bag with holes. Thus
saith the Lord of hosts; Consider your ways.*

Haggai 1:6-7

*There was a certain rich man, which had a steward; and the
same was accused unto him that he had wasted his goods.
And he called him, and said unto him ... give an account of
thy stewardship; for thou mayest be no longer steward.*

Luke 16:1-2

On my way to church service following Sunday school
one morning, John, one of my former students,
approached me. He had been through my basic money
management class about six months earlier.

"I just wanted to let you know that the lesson you gave
on how to save money on insurance was very helpful to
me," John said.

I remembered that John had been enthusiastic about
the material presented during the course.

"What part of that lesson proved beneficial?" I asked.

"When I checked on my car insurance to look for
duplication of unnecessary coverage as you suggested, I
was shocked at what I found. First of all, I had a good

company-sponsored health plan where I worked that would cover any hospital bills whether caused by an auto accident or not.

I decided to drop the duplicate coverage in my car insurance since the insurance company would not pay twice for the same medical expenses. Then by raising my deductible from $50 to $500 on comprehensive and collision, this premium also dropped."

"Great!" I said. "How much did you save?"

With a big smile, John answered, "Forty dollars per month on my car insurance alone."

"What did you do with the $40 per month that you saved?"

"I took the money and bought a new boat I couldn't afford before," John answered.

His response did not surprise me. This is the typical attitude toward spending that we should guard against as wise stewards. Chances are that John did not buy a new boat for $40. It is more likely that he bought the new boat on credit and increased his debt payments by $40 per month. Instead of adding to his surplus, he added to his monthly expenditures.

There is nothing wrong with purchasing a boat. However, one of the most common responses I receive from workshop participants across the country is that they don't have enough money to open a savings or investment account or pay down their existing debt.

This chapter will examine ways you can find money in your current budget to use for savings and investments or for your surplus account. This can be done many times with no increase in income by eliminating waste — even if you have a modest income.

GENERAL OVERVIEW

In the last chapter, we looked at how to develop the 20% surplus from existing income and how compound interest works, along with key investment strategies and how they fit into developing a sound financial plan.

In this chapter, we will look at how we can take control of our personal finances by using a family budget and thus eliminate waste from disposable income. By eliminating waste and making prudent purchases, we can make our current income go much further. Our goal is to reorganize our spending habits so that we can live on a maximum of 70% of our income after we develop our surplus.

WRITE OUT YOUR FINANCIAL GOALS

The best way to take control of your personal finances and get your financial house in order is to write out your financial goals. This process includes establishing a family budget. The family budget is a written plan that takes your existing circumstances into account — your current income and expenses. Your written plan also should include a current financial statement and list of your goals.

ESTABLISHING A FAMILY BUDGET

What is a budget? A budget is a plan of action by which you can get the maximum benefits from your existing income. It allows you to set priorities on spending.

ACTION STEP:
ESTABLISH A FAMILY BUDGET
TO SET PRIORITIES

Budgeting may not be the most anticipated activity on the family's agenda, but it is the only way that we will be able to apply biblical principles to our lives. It is the only way to put into practical application the principles of getting out of debt, saving and investing, and giving to the needy, while still being able to meet basic family needs.

Unfortunately, basic self control is not an automatic part of the average American makeup. Unless there is an organized plan for spending, the average family will have problems with over-spending.

A budget allows you to take control of personal finances. It's not the amount of money you earn that matters; it's how you manage what you have. I have talked to individuals who weren't able to make ends meet earning $12,000 per year. I have talked to individuals who could not live on $40,000 per year. And I have talked to individuals who earned over $100,000 per year who could not live on what they earned.

ACTION STEP:
LEARN TO LIVE WITHIN YOUR MEANS —
KEEP YOUR BUDGET

Learn how to live on what your earn. Yes, the secret is living within your means. As presented in Chapter 8, "Savings and Investments," you should always spend less than you make, and you will always have a surplus. Unless you implement a budget, your expenses will always outpace your income.

Budgeting allows you to take the impulse out of your spending. It allows you to develop control over spending habits.

ACTION STEP:
SET PRIORITIES FOR YOUR SPENDING
ACCORDING TO YOUR FINANCIAL GOALS
AND YOUR BUDGET

You can't have everything. You must set priorities. Budgeting must be a family effort. This will allow the family an opportunity to establish open communications in setting priorities. What are your priorities as a family? What will your number-one spending priority be? Will you put God first? What will be your second-highest priority — setting aside funds for retirement, getting out of debt or just being able to get by until next month? Set the priorities that mean most to you. Your budget allows you to take control of your circumstances instead of letting them control you.

HOW TO START YOUR BUDGET

Prepare your monthly budget, including income and a detailed list of your family's monthly expenses.

For a budget to be effective, you must use it. It must be a tool that allows you to manage your family's finances. Many people have taken the effort to start a budget but later discontinued it because of unexpected necessities, such as clothes, dentists, doctors and entertainment. (See Figures 5 and 6 in Chapter 3.)

ACTION STEP:
MAKE YOUR BUDGET AND STICK TO IT

RUNNING ALL YOUR EXPENDITURES THROUGH YOUR CHECKING ACCOUNT

To start your budget, you must determine where you are at present. What is your current situation? You must determine how much you earn and how much money you spend each month. You must keep proper records.

This step is usually the most difficult because most families tend to understate expenses. Most people don't really know what they spend each month on simple items,

such as eating out and miscellaneous expenses that aren't
payable on a monthly basis.

ACTION STEP:
RUN ALL YOUR INCOME
THROUGH YOUR CHECKING ACCOUNT

You must account for every dime spent. The easiest
way to take control of spending is to use your checking
account to pay for major purchases. Carry a small notebook
to keep track of smaller purchases. This should be done for
at least a month to establish your current spending habits
necessary to estimate your preliminary budget.

If you have a checking account, begin running all your
purchases through it. You can determine a preliminary
budget of expenses by going back through your checkbook
for one month to see where you spend your income.

HINTS FOR BALANCING THE FAMILY BUDGET

*He who puts up security for another will surely suffer, but
whoever refuses to strike hands in pledge is safe.*
Proverbs 11:15 (NIV)

*My son, if thou be surety for thy friend, if thou hast stricken
thy hand with a stranger, Thou art snared with the words
of thy mouth, thou art taken with the words of thy mouth.
Do this now, my son, and deliver thyself, when thou art
come into the hand of thy friend; go, humble thyself, and
make sure thy friend. Give not sleep to thine eyes, nor
slumber to thine eyelids. Deliver thyself as a roe from the
hand of the hunter, and as a bird from the hand of the fowler.*
Proverbs 6:1-5

A budget is in balance when income is larger than
expenditures. If you are spending more money than you
earn, your budget is out of balance. You are already in a

surety position, or you are RAPIDLY approaching this point. There are only two ways to balance a budget: increase your income or decrease your expenditures.

Regarding income, you could get a part-time job or establish a part-time business. Once you identify additional income, it is important that the extra income be applied toward getting the family budget balanced and not increasing spending.

SET FAMILY FINANCIAL GOALS TO LIVE ON 70%

The best way to involve God in your personal finances is to organize your plans according to biblical principles. Remember, the only difference between Christians and non-Christians regarding personal finances is what they are willing to do to get money and what they actually do with their money after they get it! Set a goal to live on 70% of your current income.

ACTION STEP:
SET A GOAL TO LIVE ON 70%

To establish a financial plan, set family financial goals. This can only be accomplished through communications among family members. The best way to begin this process is for the husband and wife to ask each other questions about their long-term goals and desires. What do they want to accomplish in life? They may be surprised at their answers.

ACTION STEP:
DECIDE WHERE YOU WANT TO BE
IN 5 TO 10 YEARS, AND SET
FINANCIAL GOALS TO GET THERE

I suggest you pray before you start the process, then answer the questions individually. Some sample questions are listed below. Once the questions have been answered individually, the husband and wife should come together and compare their lists. At this time there must be some adjustments and then agreement must take place. If either spouse is too far out, that person should drop back to a point where both can agree. No decisions on spending money should be made unless both partners are in agreement on the purchase. If no agreement is reached, no purchase should be made. Husbands and wives should, of course, be supportive of each other. Remember that the purpose of this exercise is to bring the family closer together in order to accomplish financial objectives.

Some sample questions follow:

PERSONAL FINANCIAL GOALS

1. What are the most important things that you would like to accomplish?

2. What long-term financial goals would you like to achieve in 10 to 20 years? How much do you want to set aside for long-term savings?

3. What financial goals would you like to achieve within the next 5 to 10 years?

4. What financial goals would you like to finish next year?

5. Do you communicate clearly with your spouse about financial matters?

6. What are your educational plans for the children?

7. What are your retirement goals?

8. What are your giving goals (to the Gospel and the poor)?

9. What are your goals concerning debt and interest payments?

10. What do you want to give to your local church?

A WRITTEN PLAN

ACTION STEP:
PUT YOUR FINANCIAL GOALS IN WRITING

Your goals should be written to get the best results:

And the Lord answered me, and said, Write the vision, and make it plain upon tables, that he may run that readeth it.
Habakkuk 2:2

Moreover, they should be prepared with input from the entire family. By establishing written goals, your family will learn how to set priorities. The process will allow you to identify the objectives that you feel are most important to the family. These exercises will help bring the family closer together, establishing a solid channel of communication between husband and wife. Furthermore, with input from the children parents can identify realistic family goals and put everyone on the same track.

There are several things you should do in establishing your family goals:

1. Understand fundamental biblical principles that govern your finances. Then these principles should be incorporated as you organize your overall goals. (See "20 Key Strategies To Eliminating Waste and Building a Sound Financial Foundation" in Chapter 8.)

2. Husband and wife should write out individual goals separately. Then the children should do the same.

3. After each individual writes his or her personal goals, the husband and wife should compile the family goals.

Make your goals practical and realistic. Examples of goals that you and your family may want to accomplish are:

- Buying a new house
- College for the children
- Having a retirement fund
- Buying a new automobile

These goals may be divided into long-term and short-term ones. One goal may be of higher priority to the family than another.

Each family member should have an opportunity to provide input in establishing priorities for your family goals. After the input from other members of the family, the husband and wife should set final priorities.

Be realistic in establishing goals. Make them practical. Don't make them unrealistic. If you set your goals too far out into the future, where you really don't believe you can accomplish them, they are unrealistic and will hinder your overall financial plan.

Then take your long-term and intermediate goals and break them into bite-sized chunks, which can be handled on a month-to-month basis.

And finally, we should use a daily "Things To Do" list. This list of things should consist of what comes up during the week, but priority should be given to items consistent with your longer-term and intermediate goals.

MORE HINTS ON BALANCING THE BUDGET

The best way to reduce the amount of money you spend each month is to divide each category into separate components and then identify ways to reduce spending in each area. The main areas of expense are:

- Housing
- Food
- Transportation (car purchase and upkeep)
- Clothing
- Insurance and Medical Expenses
- Entertainment and Recreation
- Miscellaneous
- Debt reduction

• **Housing:** The following list of items can reduce your expenses for shelter. The expenses in this category are house payments, maintenance, lawn upkeep, taxes and insurance, telephone and other utilities. Your housing expenses should be between 25 and 30% of your net income.

1. When purchasing a home, the best buy is an older house or foreclosure. Make sure your house is adequate for your living needs today; but don't buy a house that is larger than you need, with plans to expand into it.

2. Examine your interest rate and refinance if there are two points or more between it and the current rate. For example, if you have a 30-year mortgage at 10.5% for $100,000, you can save more than $200 per month through refinancing at 8 to 8 1/2%. You also can purchase a 15-year mortgage for a few dollars more per month. Check with your local mortgage company for options.

3. Consider doing maintenance and upkeep yourself — lawn care, pest control, painting and carpet cleaning.

4. Examine your current homeowners' insurance and compare the price with three other insurance companies. Increasing your deductible could substantially reduce your premium.

5. Lower your utility bills by installing ceiling fans and limiting use of heating, lights and air conditioning.

6. Never buy furniture and appliances on credit when trying to reduce your expenses. Use garage sales and used appliance stores to get reasonable prices on household goods and appliances or pay for them with cash from your surplus account. Newspaper ads are also a source to locate good buys.

7. Write letters instead of making long-distance phone calls.

• **Food:** Groceries, sundry items and eating out. Food expenses should not exceed 15 to 20% of the family budget. This item requires definite planning to reap benefits.

1. The best way to cut food expenses is to decide on a daily menu at least for an entire week.

2. Once you have established what you will serve, make a list of items that will support the menu. When you go shopping, always use a written list to avoid impulse buying.

3. Make your grocery list for an entire week to conserve gas and limit unnecessary trips to the market. Reduce or eliminate ready-to-eat items, such as sugar-coated cereal, TV dinners, pot pies and cakes.

4. Avoid going shopping when you are hungry. Leave children and hungry spouses at home; they will always pressure you to buy things that are not on your list.

5. Always pay attention as the clerk rings up the items in your basket; then double-check your receipt when you get home. If an item does not ring up correctly, bring it to the attention of the store manager. Sale prices are sometimes left out of the store's computer.

6. Consider canning fresh fruits and vegetables whenever possible. Save glass jars from products you buy for this purpose.

7. Make lunches for your spouse and children to reduce lunch expenses.

8. Reduce use of disposable items, such as paper towels, plates, cups and napkins. These incidentals can be more expensive than you think.

• **Transportation:** Automobile payments, gasoline and maintenance. This category should not exceed 10 to 15% of your net income. The main purpose of an automobile is transportation. Many families, however, have been trapped into buying cars they cannot afford because they view automobiles as status symbols.

1. Keep the automobile you have. It is better to repair an automobile that still has miles of use than to purchase a new one and be locked into monthly payments. The average American car will last from five to seven years with proper maintenance. Many will last longer.

2. Buy a low-cost used car and drive it until it can no longer be maintained inexpensively.

3. Take care of your automobile. Change the oil every 2,500 to 3,000 miles, especially in city driving.

4. When purchasing a new automobile, it is best to wait for year-end sales.

5. Purchase a two-year-old car from a wholesaler. Look for a model that maintains body style for a number of years. Usually this process will allow you to have a low-mileage car at up to 50% of its original value.

6. Pay cash for your car when possible. Use your short-term savings account (surplus account) to accumulate the cash.

7. Never take credit-life insurance when financing a car. It is more than 500% higher than purchasing insurance directly from the insurance company.

• **Clothing:** This category should not exceed 4 to 5% of your net income. Many families with limited income spend more money than they should in this area. Many families are held hostage by fads. Sporting outfits, for example, are astronomically priced.

1. Make an annual budget for clothing needs. Make a list of items you need and purchase them in the off-season. Shop at economical and off-price stores and garage sales. You can end up with designer labels at a good price if you shop carefully.

2. Educate family members on caring for their clothing and other possessions. Teach everyone how to do the laundry to keep clothing in shape.

• **Insurance and Medical Expenses:**

1. Never take the minimum $50 to $100 deductible on your insurance. Increase your deductible to $500 or $1,000 dollars and save as much as 50% on automobile insurance.

2. On health insurance, use your company's group policy when possible. Use a higher deductible to cut costs and still be covered for major illness. Cover the higher deductible out of your emergency funds in your surplus account.

3. Practice preventive medicine. It is much better to maintain a healthy body than to pay additional money on doctor bills. See that you and your family practice proper nutrition, exercise and get enough rest. Get regular checkups and recommended tests at the appropriate ages.

4. Reduce dental bills by practicing proper dental hygiene and having regular checkups. Take care of minor problems before they become major ones.

NOTE: A more detailed discussion on insurance will follow this discussion.

• **Entertainment and Recreation**: This category covers vacation and recreational activities. You should not spend more than 3 to 5% of your spendable income on this area of your budget.

1. Plan to take vacations during off-seasons. This will significantly reduce the cost.

2. In an effort to reduce recreational spending, arrange vacations closer to home or in less trendy spots.

3. Consider the possibility of taking camping vacations to avoid motel and restaurant expenses. When you do stay in a motel, pack the ice chest and eat one meal per day in your room.

4. Vacation packages often offer the best buys. Many include transportation, room and some meals.

5. When taking children along, remember that many educational activities, such as visiting museums, parks and historical sites, are fun and inexpensive.

• **Miscellaneous:** Gifts, entertainment, school expenses and allowances. This category should take no more than 3 to 5% of your income.

1. When purchasing gifts for Christmas, have the family agree on limits. Ask relatives to give cash you can put on debt principal instead of gifts.

2. Purchase gifts, Christmas and other holiday items during off-seasons and stash them in a closet until needed. Gifts can be pre-wrapped and labeled for "emergencies."

3. Set allowances for adults and children. This area is a real budget buster; therefore, it is necessary to make provisions at budget-setting time for husband and wife to have money to spend on personal items.

• **Debt Reduction:** This part of your expenses should not consume more than 10% of your income for interest and principal payments.

1. Establish a debt-reduction plan, and set a goal to eliminate interest payments.

2. Pay all credit cards in full at the end of each month or destroy them.

3. Always avoid surety in your personal finances. If you make $12,000 or less, you can't afford to purchase items

on credit. Principal and interest payments are sure budget busters.

HOW TO SAVE 50% TO 70% ON YOUR INSURANCE

Earlier, it is stated that the average individual can reduce insurance costs by as much as 50%. This chapter will explain how.

First of all, we should remember that the purpose of insurance is to act as a safety net, not as protection. Your protection is in the Lord (Psalm 91). Insurance should be purchased to repair or replace damaged or lost property. Life insurance should be used to replace the income of the major breadwinner in case of death.

Most insurance is sold through fear. "If something should happen, you would want to protect your loved ones, wouldn't you?" the salesperson asks. The more you think about the consequences from an emotional standpoint, the more insurance you purchase that you don't really need.

With a closer look at the facts, we can eliminate much of the confusion regarding insurance. Many families spend up to one-third of their income on interest and insurance. But your total insurance cost need not be more than 5% of your total income.

Insurance can be divided into these categories: auto, life, home-owners', health and others. Following is a look at each type.

AUTOMOBILE INSURANCE

Automobile insurance can be one of the most costly areas. It is a part of casualty insurance, a term which covers everything other than life insurance. There are three basic areas of automobile insurance: liability, comprehensive and collision.

• **Liability Insurance:** Liability insurance covers damages to someone else's person or property. If you were to accidentally hit someone's automobile, your liability policy would pay to repair the other person's car. If someone was hurt, it would cover treatment of that person's injuries. There are three fundamental types of liability insurance: bodily injury, property damage liability and umbrella liability.

• **Bodily Injury Liability Insurance:** This bodily injury liability insurance covers people in the other car in an accident, the policyholder and passengers in the policy-holder's car when driving someone else's car or a rental car. Bodily injury insurance also covers legal defense damage up to the limit of the policy.

Most states require a minimum of $10,000/$20,000 in liability coverage. This means that the policyholder is covered $10,000 per person up to a maximum of $20,000 per accident.

How much bodily liability insurance should you carry? The average may vary from family to family. If you rent and don't own any property and live from paycheck to paycheck, you probably can get by with the minimum. If you have $50,000 to $100,000 equity in your home, personal assets, retirement accounts, etc., you might want to consider increasing that coverage to $250,000/$500,000.

• **Property Damage Liability:** How much property damage liability should you cover? Remember, property damage liability covers damages to someone else's car or property caused by the policyholder's car. This insurance covers your family and anyone to whom you have given permission to drive your car. To properly cover yourself, you should consider the current cost of automobiles and the cost of two or three (in case of a pile-up). You should consider a minimum of at least $50,000 or a maximum of $100,000 per accident.

In most cases, you will pay higher premiums if there is a teenage male driver in your family.

• **Umbrella Liability Policies:** What about umbrella liability coverage? This is a liability policy sold by home and automobile insurance companies.

Because of high costs of court and the proliferation of lawsuits, everyone with reasonable assets is concerned about a lawsuit. Yet in most cases, your insurance agent won't mention an umbrella policy to you because it is so inexpensive and pays a small commission. It varies from company to company, but the cost is usually between $100 and $150 per year for $1 million worth of coverage. Usually you get the best price when you get both homeowner's and auto insurance from the same company issuing the umbrella policy. You should have $100,000 to $300,000 in coverage. Instead of doubling the coverage on both your home and auto insurance, you should add a $100,000 umbrella policy to complete your liability coverage.

• **Comprehensive Automobile Insurance:** This policy takes up where the liability policy leaves off. While liability insurance takes care of damage or injury to someone's car or property, comprehensive insurance covers your own car or property.

Comprehensive insurance pays for losses such as theft, fire damage, windshield and glass breakage, hail damage and damage from falling objects. The minimum deductible ranges from $50 to $100, depending on the company.

• **Collision Automobile Insurance:** This insurance also covers damage to your car. No matter who is at fault, if you collide with another vehicle, you will be covered under a collision package. If the other driver is at fault, however, your insurance company will seek reimbursement from the other driver's insurance company. The deductible for this collision insurance ranges from $100 to $1,000.

HOW TO SAVE 40% to 50% ON
YOUR AUTOMOBILE INSURANCE

There are many different ways to cut slices from your automobile insurance. The major ways are outlined below.

1. Increase your deductible on your comprehensive coverage from the standard $50 to $500. You will save as much as 30% in some cases.

2. Avoid double coverage. You cannot collect twice on the same medical expenses, no matter how many insurance companies cover you.

3. Avoid uninsured motorist coverage. This is usually a duplicate coverage since any damage done to your auto will be covered by your auto insurance and any bodily injury will be covered by your hospitalization policy.

4. Avoid no-fault insurance unless it is required by the state in which you live. This is often a double-coverage insurance.

5. Drop insurance you don't need. When your car drops below a certain value, your insurance company will pay you only the market value no matter how much you pay for comprehensive and collision. It's cheaper to insure it yourself.

6. Avoid rental car insurance. Rental car insurance is often covered on your credit card, and you are covered under your auto insurance and hospitalization. Rental car insurance is almost always double coverage.

7. Avoid special TV and mail-order insurance. Most mail-order insurance is expensive. It is usually marked up 400% to 500% to cover expensive advertising.

8. Avoid extended warranties. Extended warranties are available from retail outlets for automobiles and some appliances. These insurance policies normally cover your appliances or car through the warranty period or a certain length of time. You should look at this type of coverage and make up your own mind. It is normally expensive and, in many cases, never used. But I have seen cases on some new appliances and ice-maker refrigerators when this warranty has come in handy. For the most part, you will save money by eliminating extended warranties on most household products.

> ### *ACTION STEP:*
> ### *ASK FOR AUTOMOBILE*
> ### *INSURANCE DISCOUNTS*

[For more detailed information, enroll in the Stewardship in Action — Small Group Study Course. For more information on the course, call (501) 834-1168.]

DROPPED OR LAPSED POLICIES

It is very important not to let your auto policy lapse or drop your coverage before you establish coverage with another company.

An example from my own life applies. When our family had an unexpected reduction in income, we cut everything to the bare necessities. We decided to let our automobile insurance premium slide for a few months.

As business picked up again, we went back to our insurance company to reinstate coverage on our automobiles. When we contacted our agent, he informed us that we could not renew our policy under previous conditions. When I asked why not, he said that it had been more than 30 days since the policy expired. Therefore, I would have to start up as a new customer with no previous insurance record.

"Okay," I said, "What is the additional cost going to be?"

"That will be $1,200 for the first six months," he said.

"What! $1,200?" I said. "Our policy was only $275 for six months before. Are you telling me that the cost of the same policy will increase more than 400% even though I have the same clean driving record?"

"Yes, that is the way it is," he said. "You will have to pay this insurance premium for the first year, and then your insurance premium will decrease by 10% if you maintain a good driving record."

Needless to say, I was extremely disturbed over this development. It would have been better for me to have dropped all other coverage and kept simple liability on my automobile than to drop all coverage. The same principle applies if you have a series of accidents or traffic violations because your rates will skyrocket.

CHOOSE YOUR INSURANCE AGENT WISELY

In many cases, people buy insurance from a person they know and trust. They feel this person is looking out for their best interests. They feel the agent understands their situation.

However, if you do not know your options and you let your guard down, the temptation for the agent to make a commission is much too great. The agent often will sell you the policy that will make the most commission for the salesperson and long-term cash flow for the company.

A wise steward understands how the system works and shops around to keep insurance and investment brokers honest. A wise steward tells his or her dollars where to go and pays only a fair commission for services needed.

I suggest you get a financial adviser or broker who understands both insurance (automobile and life) and investments (no-load mutual funds). See Chapter 8 for guidelines in choosing this adviser.

LIFE INSURANCE

SAVE UP TO 70% ON LIFE INSURANCE

Insurance is often poorly defined for individuals at the time of purchase. Consequently, many Americans spend much more than they should. Overspending on insurance combined with interest on debt could consume as much as one third of the average family income. Of course, this amount may vary among families. Yet many individuals who purchase insurance primarily take the word of their agent and usually buy more than they need. This section will take a closer look at life insurance to see where waste can be eliminated.

Life insurance is an institutional plan by which an insurance company allows you to pay certain amounts of money while you are living so that you can leave money to your loved ones after you die. The main purpose of life insurance is to protect your family or loved ones from financial disaster if you should die. You want them to live basically the same lifestyle they had before your death.

Life insurance is excellent for this purpose, but you must understand how basic life insurance works to meet this purpose wisely. Following are some of the basic terms associated with life insurance. Knowing these terms will help you understand how to make proper decisions regarding life insurance.

• **Death Benefits:** The amount of money the insurance company will pay the beneficiary when the insured person dies. This also is called the face value of the insurance policy. This is the amount of life insurance proceeds that will be received by your loved ones.

• **Term of the Policy:** The time period for which the life insurance is in force. The term of the policy can be any amount of time (one year, ten years, 20 years, lifetime).

• **Premium:** The money you pay the insurance company to have the life insurance policy in force. These premiums can be paid in a number of different ways — monthly, semi-annually, annually and sometimes in lump sum single premiums. Most policies fall into the quarterly or monthly categories.

There are at least four instances in which you should not purchase life insurance:

• You should never buy insurance on children.

• If you have no dependents and no assets, you do not need life insurance.

• Do not buy education policies for your children.

• You should never purchase life insurance as an investment.

INSURANCE ON CHILDREN

Regarding life insurance for children, you should remember the purpose of the insurance is to protect your family against loss of your financial assets when you die. Children are not financial assets.

Many parents are persuaded to buy life insurance on their children by salespeople they feel know best. And these salespeople often tell parents that buying insurance for their children is a responsible thing to do. The usual line is, "You love your children, don't you? Therefore, you should insure them."

The main point that the salesperson does not mention is that the longer you are in a whole life policy, the more money the company and salesperson make. The longer a person lives, the more insurance premiums he or she pays. Salespeople will tell you that you should insure children while they are young so that they will be guaranteed to be eligible for insurance later. Yet, according to statistics, more than 99% of teenagers are eligible for insurance at age 18.

INDIVIDUAL INSURANCE WITH NO DEPENDENTS AND NO ASSETS

Looking at the statistics, we find that about 30% of the life insurance policies in effect are on the lives of unmarried people with no family obligations. They have purchased insurance because insurance companies have convinced them that everyone should have life insurance.

Life insurance should be used to prevent financial loss and hardship to the beneficiary after a person dies. Why would a young person who has no dependents or family buy a life insurance policy? To whom would he or she leave the proceeds?

Remember that the purpose of life insurance is to protect the ones who are left. It would be more appropriate for young people to invest in a mutual fund that would produce more interest income and give them coverage for funeral expenses if something unexpected happened.

INSURANCE POLICY FOR COLLEGE

Regarding a child's education, a life insurance policy is one of the lowest interest-paying investment accounts. You should never mix investment and insurance in the same package. The insurance company will always win. For example, if you started with a $100,000 life insurance policy on your newborn child, it would be worth approximately $12,000 when the child reached college age. This policy would cost you $500 per month. On the other hand, if you had taken the same $500 a month and put it into a mutual fund family, you would create a college fund of more than $90,000 over the same amount of time.

Never use insurance as an investment. The same is true for any insurance purchase, whether it is for your child's education, your retirement or any other financial benefit. When you buy a life insurance policy, you should buy it solely for life insurance.

HOW TO SAVE UP TO 80% ON YOUR LIFE INSURANCE

To be able to save on your life insurance, you must understand three types available:

1. Whole Life

2. Universal Life

3. Term Life

1. Whole Life Insurance is the insurance responsible for leading thousands, if not millions, of individuals to invest in insurance policies instead of buying straight term insurance.

Whole life insurance is a plan in which you can receive cash value at the same time as receiving insurance coverage. This type of insurance sometimes has a 300 to 400% markup over term insurance.

Whole life policies can be dressed up or down, depending on what the individual wants to achieve and the information given by the salesperson. Whole life policies usually have level premiums and claim to build tax-deferred cash value. Tax-deferred cash value is a nice sounding term, but it has no value whatsoever to the insured. When you die, the cash value remains with the insurance company. The beneficiary receives only the policy's face value.

There are a number of marketing gimmicks used when whole life is presented. Once you take a look at the major promises and examine actual results, you see in most cases that whole life is not a sound purchase for most individuals. Below are a few misleading claims concerning whole life insurance:

• **You can borrow against your cash value.** With whole life insurance, as your cash value grows, the insurance company tells you that you can borrow against your cash value at low interest rates. This sounds good, but actually the insurance company is charging you interest on your own money. Moreover, if you borrow against your life insurance policy and do not repay the loan, it will be deducted from your death benefit.

• **You earn interest on your insurance policy.** Through examining whole life insurance, you find that the interest rate is normally the lowest in the financial market — normally between 1 and 2% (sometimes as high as 3%, depending on the market rate). Nevertheless, this is a benefit, or is it? As we indicated earlier, cash value remains with the insurance company if you should die. The interest that you receive goes toward the cash value, not to the beneficiary whom you intended. This is another reason why you should not use insurance as an investment. If you want to earn interest, it would be better to invest in a no-load stock or bond fund.

• **Your policy will eventually be a paid-up insurance policy.** Salespeople will tell you that if you pay a certain amount of money into your policy, you will have a paid-up policy. This means you no longer will have to pay premiums to maintain your insurance policy. You will have insurance without premiums.

Take a closer look at paid-up policies. To receive one, you have to pay your premium for several years. The money you overpaid your insurance will be used at some point in time by the insurance company to pay your premiums. In essence, what you have done is to put in enough money that the interest will pay your premiums. You could have had a much better return if you had invested your own money.

• **Your insurance is a tax shelter.** The implication here is that life insurance has some type of special tax benefits. The salesperson will tell you that you can borrow money from your insurance policy tax free. Big deal! Anytime you borrow money from the bank or any other place, it is always tax free. Borrowed money has no income tax; therefore, this is a completely invalid statement.

Insurance companies also claim that all life insurance benefits upon your death are tax exempt. In fact, after a person dies there is no income tax on any part of that person's property. However, insurance benefits and the other part of the estate are subject to estate taxes. You are led to believe that the insurance company has something to do with tax benefits, but it does not.

• **Buy insurance while you are young and save money.** Insurance premiums are lower when you are younger, but the longer you pay into the insurance company, the more money the insurance company makes. Money can be a progressive asset if it is properly invested.

Remember that the purpose of insurance is to protect your financial assets for your family after you die. If you don't have any assets, there is no need for life insurance.

2. Universal Life Insurance is much like whole life in the sense that it has many hidden charges that keep the money with the insurance company. Universal life is a term life policy basically, with some type of investment plan included. The investment part of the policy is flexible to the extent you can use different types of investment vehicles. The investment part of the premium can be set up in a fixed-rate account or be self-directed into some type of mutual fund.

The way universal life insurance works is that the premium cost is set above the insurance cost. Once the premium and other charges have been paid, the balance of your money goes into the investment. Because of the high cost of insurance fees and commissions, only a portion of your money ever gets to the investment account.

Usually you are told that you are getting a guaranteed rate on your money. In reality, you only get the guaranteed rate on the money that actually gets to the investment account.

For example, a person buys a universal life policy with a $100,000 death benefit and is promised a 10% return for 20 years. Suppose the premium is $2,000 per year. Then the insured is paid only on the money that goes into the investment account, assuming that the person starts the first year by paying the $2,000 premium. Then fees and the cost of insurance are deducted from this premium amount. It is possible that 30% of the $2,000 will be deducted just to open the account. In other words, instead of investing $2,000, the insured has only $1,400 left to go into the investment account.

In addition, this investment probably will earn less than 6% per year. Each year the policy carries other hidden costs, and the cost of the term insurance also is going up each year, both further reducing the amount that goes into your investment account. Most people never recognize these extra charges and fees because their premium stays the same.

Watch out for the fine print. Universal life policies may state that they will pay you a guaranteed 10%, but if you take your money out of the policy, the amount of proceeds can drop as much as 50%.

ACTION STEP:
USE THE 21 PRACTICAL STEP PLAN TO GET
A HIGHER RETURN ON YOUR INVESTMENT
INSTEAD OF BUYING LOW-INTEREST
INSURANCE POLICIES (SEE CHAPTER 12)

---

3. Term Life Insurance is the life insurance people should be buying instead of whole life or universal life. This is the actual insurance with no investment plans or hidden charges.

Term insurance is the least expensive of all life insurance. It is many times as low as 80% of the cost of whole life or universal life.

As stated earlier, you should not combine insurance and investment into one package. If there is an insurance need, I suggest that you purchase term life and take the balance and put it into a mutual fund.

BUY TERM LIFE INSURANCE
AND SAVE THE DIFFERENCE

There are three types of term insurance:

• **Annual renewal term:** A policy is purchased for a period of one year. At the end of that year, you receive a statement so that you can renew the policy for another year.

The insurance increases a few dollars each year, but the insurance is guaranteed renewable every year if you pay your premium. This is perhaps the best type of insurance for a growing family.

• **Decreasing term insurance:** This type allows you to pay premiums that remain the same, but the amount of the insurance decreases. Decreasing term is used primarily as mortgage insurance to cover homes and other items for which you want the insurance benefit to drop after the product that is financed is paid off.

• **Level premium term:** This type allows you to choose a policy for 5, 10 or 15 years with your premium and the amount of insurance remaining the same. With level term you will pay more for the premium in the early years, but the difference balances out over the term of the policy.

SUMMARIZING INSURANCE

As we have seen, there are many types of insurance. They all have a purpose. The cost varies from one insurance company to the other.

Eliminate waste whenever you can. You should examine your policies — and not depend on the agent or insurance company — to make sure that the coverage is right for you.

ACTION STEP:
ALWAYS MAKE SURE YOU HAVE A REPLACEMENT
POLICY WITH A BETTER OVERALL RETURN
BEFORE YOU CANCEL ANY EXISTING POLICY

Look at the various types of insurance available in the following chart. If you use this information in conjunction with what has been presented in this chapter, you can reduce your overall insurance costs.

Figure 9

TYPE OF INSURANCE	BEFORE	AFTER	NET SAVINGS
Auto	$1,500	$ 800	+ $ 700
Whole Life	1,500	0	+ 1,500
Universal Life	0	0	0
Term Life	0	360	- 360
Debit Life	225	0	+ 225
Cancer & Specialty	250	0	+ 250
Mortgage	700	375	+ 325
Hospital	1,500	1,000	+ 500
Disability	500	0	+ 500
Homeowner's	400	300	+ 100
Umbrella	0	160	- 160

HOW TO SAVE ON TAXES

Individuals must be responsible for carrying out appropriate research into tax laws and keeping necessary records, while feeling comfortable with the actions they are taking. Christians, furthermore, must handle business affairs with honesty and integrity always.

Obviously tax reduction is a complex area, which cannot be covered in detail here. But the two areas that follow are excellent steps that the average family can take which will have a direct impact on their tax burden:

1. IRA (Individual Retirement Account): The average family is allowed to take $2,000 off the top of their income and put it directly into a retirement account. With a few restrictions, this transition is completely tax-deferred for the average wage earner. For example, if you earn $20,000 per year, you will pay tax on only $18,000 for the year you invest $2,000 in an IRA. If you select a reputable no-load or rear-load mutual fund, your retirement account will receive compound interest on the pre-tax dollar until you retire. (See Chapter 8.)

2. Small Business Deductions: If you start and operate a small business, you are allowed to deduct the expenses of the business. It is important that you understand the tax regulations and be willing to keep proper records. Check with your local IRS office for their circular on small businesses.

CONCLUSION

Many Americans have been caught in the trap of wasting financial resources without ever realizing it through impulse buying. Because of the Madison Avenue mentality, we are not only buying things on impulse, but we are buying things that we don't really need; and we are paying too much for them because of the use of credit.

It is not the amount of money you bring in but the amount of money you keep that counts. It is how much you can reduce your current expenditures over the amount that you earn.

Impulse buying is a sign of lack of discipline and self-control over lust and personal desires. This habit is a true indicator of the power and control that the world economy has over our lives.

ACTION STEP:
GET OUT OF A SURETY POSITION:
ESTABLISH A SURPLUS ACCOUNT

To eliminate waste, you must reduce your current spending habits to establish a surplus. You should set the direction in which your money flows — not the Madison

Avenue advertiser, your friends and neighbors, or any set of false attitudes that presently define success in your life. Your standards of success should be defined by God's Word.

If, after examining your budget, you find yourself in a surety position, you must change your spending habits. If your expenses exceed your income, you are already in a surety position, or you are rapidly heading in that direction. If the market value of your assets is less than what you owe, you are in a surety position! The first step to getting your financial house in order is to establish a plan to get out of a surety position.

If you are truly serious about applying biblical money management principles to your personal finances, I suggest the following:

1. Ask your pastor to set up classes to teach biblical principles for basic money management.

2. Let your church select a person who will take this on as a ministry.

3. Contact Urban Ministries for a brochure on how to start the Stewardship in Action — Small Group Study Course at your church.

PRACTICAL APPLICATION

1. Review the "Type of Insurance" chart (Figure 9) in this chapter and examine your current insurance policies against this chart.

2. Use the "21 Practical Steps to Build Wealth in God's Economy" in Chapter 12 to organize your financial plan.

3. If you would like assistance putting your plan into operation, contact Urban Ministries for a catalog of support materials.

10

TRAINING YOUR CHILDREN TO MANAGE MONEY
ENSURE THEIR FINANCIAL FUTURE

Train up a child in the way he should go: and when he is old, he will not depart from it.

Proverbs 22:6

Therefore shall ye lay up these my words in your heart and in your soul, and bind them for a sign upon your hand, that they may be as frontlets between your eyes. And ye shall teach them your children, speaking of them when thou sittest in thine house, and when thou walkest by the way, when thou liest down, and when thou risest up. And thou shalt write them upon the door posts of thine house, and upon thy gates: That your days may be multiplied, and the days of your children, in the land which the Lord sware unto your fathers to give them, as the days of heaven upon the earth.

Deuteronomy 11:18-21

Richard told me a sad story of his grandfather, who once had owned 2,800 acres of prime timberland in Alabama. "My grandfather died at age 55," he said. "He lived most of his life as a logger. He had seven children, five boys and two girls. One of the boys died early, which left six children. My grandfather was thought to be a good businessman even though he lived in a small town.

"Over the years working with his sons, he accumulated this large tract of land. He bought the land, cut and sold the timber and paid for the land, one tract at a time. He continued until he owned 2,800 acres, and over the years his land appreciated in value because of a hunting camp he had opened on the Dog River."

As Richard continued, he explained why he thought it was important for a family to organize their financial affairs. "My grandfather's main possession was his property. When he died unexpectedly and without a will, my grandmother did not receive full ownership of the property. She received an equal share with the children.

"Grandmother loved all of her children and could not decide what was the best way to proceed. Every time the family talked about how to divide the land to try to keep the property in the family, no plan ever materialized.

"One recommendation was to take the plots and divide them into seven parcels and let each child draw a number. This did not work because they all feared they might draw the lowlands and this would be unfair.

"Since they could not agree on any settlement, they were forced to sell the land. Grandmother was allowed to keep the homestead. The money was divided equally between my father and his brothers and sisters.

"This turned out to be one of the worst options but seemed the only way to settle the matter. Within five years, the two sisters used their shares to buy homes in Detroit. Two of the brothers bought property in other locations. The other two unwisely spent their shares of the money and went completely broke."

As Richard concluded his story, I was taken with harsh reality, but at the same time realized that many similar cases exist. "At every family meeting," Richard said, "there were arguments about the property. The equal shares scenario totally split the family apart. No one had controlling authority. The bad thing about this whole situation was that seven years later they discovered oil on the tract next to Dog River."

From this example, we see that Richard's grandfather was a hard worker, good provider, and wanted the best for his family. Even though he was all of these things, he never made provisions for his property, nor taught his children how to manage it. Consequently, his lifetime possessions were not directed the way he had intended and that was to stay in the family for its benefit.

TRAINING YOUR CHILDREN

Train up a child in the way he should go: and when he is old, he will not depart from it.

Proverbs 22:6

It is our responsibility as parents to teach our children how to handle money. Most children do not start to learn how to handle money until after they leave home.

The best training for your children is to develop and implement good money management skills early in life. Children learn many personal skills in the early years of their lives from observing how their parents do things. Therefore, it is necessary for you, as a parent, to give your children a good model to emulate. To teach them how to manage money according to biblical guidelines, you must first learn how to apply the biblical principles in your own life.

Parents must realize that their attitudes and ways of spending money greatly influence children. By being a good example in the way they handle money, parents train their children to become good stewards over the resources with which they are entrusted.

BUDGETING

An allowance will give a child the opportunity to handle his or her own money. Usually a child is ready to receive an allowance even before beginning school.

Through an allowance, a child is given a certain amount of money per week as his or her share of the family income. In turn, the child is assigned various chores to help the family's work. If the work is not completed, the child does not receive any allowance.

The amount of the weekly allowance depends upon the child's age, their needs and the financial circumstances of the family. The most important thing is not the amount of allowance given, but that a child learns to be responsible in handling money.

Parents may give advice and guidance on how to handle money, but a child has to have the freedom to decide how to spend the allowance. In the end, the child must learn to make the final decision. This will enable the child to learn by trial and error. When a child finds that spending his or her whole allowance on a single item, such as a bag of popcorn, means the child will have to wait a whole week before buying something else, the youngster starts to watch spending more closely. The child will begin to examine the need to buy or to save. As the child grows, their capability of handling money coming in as an allowance also matures and the amount may be gradually increased.

THE THREE-JAR METHOD

When teaching a child to budget, begin by teaching the child the impact of learning how to live off 70% of income. I believe the best way to do this is by the "Three-Jar Method." Set up three jars labeled by category — 10% giving (tithes), 10% short-term savings and 10% long-term savings. This teaches the child to save and pay cash for what he or she wants to buy. From the very beginning, the remaining 70% is the money the child may use to spend on whatever he or she wants to purchase. Each week as the allowance is given, the child deposits a portion into each jar. Even a young child can understand this procedure because when there is no more money to spend, the 70% jar is empty.

The way my 10-year-old daughter handled her allowance was to give 10% to the church, place 20% in her bank savings account and save 70% in a special place. She then asked my wife to buy the smaller things she needed. Many times she ended up with almost 90% of her money in savings.

As she grew older, she began to realize the advantage of saving to have money to spend when everyone else was out of money. When training a child to budget, the objective should be to gradually increase responsibility until the child is independent in managing money.

From the time our children were 6 years old, they understood the Three-Jar Method. Although my son took his 10% to church and stuffed the 20% long-term savings and short-term savings in the same jar, he still maintained the concept. The problem, however, was that he would spend every dime he got his hands on over the 30%. My son, like many other young people, began to develop an appetite for brand-name tennis shoes and designer jeans. Although he had been faithful in setting aside the 30%, he seemed not to be developing in some of the other financial areas.

One day I discussed this point with my wife. I said, "If we allow him the opportunity to purchase his own tennis shoes and clothes, then he will make better choices about spending." We decided that the incentive would be to let him keep the money he saved.

We noticed that this began to have an immediate impact. He began to be more responsible in his spending habits. He began to buy less expensive items and keep the difference.

Thus we decided to let him have his own checking account to pay for such things as clothes, school supplies and tuition. We assisted him in setting up the right account with no monthly fees or service charges. We explained that if he maintained the account properly (no bounced checks), he would receive a significant increase in his allowance. I showed him how to balance his account each month and explained the cost of a bounced check.

Our son has become aware of every dime that goes through his checking account. He balances his checkbook each month and knows how much money he has to spend. This maturity came as a result of our increasing his income and responsibilities when he was faithful with smaller amounts.

ESTABLISHING AN ATTITUDE OF GIVING

The best way to establish an attitude of giving is when a child is young. This works best when children are allowed to give and can tangibly see where their giving is beneficial. A child will better understand the impact of giving when they contribute in ways such as helping support orphans, buying food for the needy and homeless, or giving offerings to missions.

It is also good for children to participate in a family prayer time each week for worship and dedicating the weeks' gifts to the Lord.

SHOULD YOU GIVE CHILDREN MONEY TO GIVE TO THE CHURCH?

In my opinion, giving is a part of worship to God. When I was growing up, I used to sit next to my mother in church, wiggling like any other five-year-old. But when the offering plate would come by, my mother would take a coin and let me drop it into the plate. After the plate was gone, I was back to my own regular activities, not realizing any special significance.

Instead of giving a child a coin to drop into the offering plate, I believe the best way to train children to be faithful is to give them something with which to be faithful. Give them an allowance and teach them the importance of making a contribution to an offering. Teach them to use 10% of their money as an offering in worship to God. Lead them to understand that they are giving this out of obedience and love to Him.

This teaching should be based on the biblical principle we learned in Chapter 3: "Planning and Preparation." All that we have belongs to God, and while we are here on earth, He is allowing us to take care of it (to be stewards of it). Therefore, we are to use it wisely.

11

FAITH FOR GOD'S SUPERNATURAL INCREASE
CHANGING EXISTING CIRCUMSTANCES

Whosoever shall say unto this mountain, Be thou removed, and be thou cast into the sea; and shall not doubt in his heart, but shall believe that those things which he saith shall come to pass; he shall have whatsoever he saith. Therefore I say unto you, What things soever ye desire, when ye pray, believe that ye receive them, and ye shall have them.

Mark 11:23-24

And God is able to make all grace abound toward you; that ye always having all sufficiency in all things, may abound to every good work.

II Corinthians 9:8

Faith can change financial circumstances. The first step of faith is to believe you can do what God says you can do and that you can have what God says you can have.

God operates a fail-safe financial system stacked in favor of the believer. However, you first must learn how to get the most out of what you have. You must be a good steward and manage what you have already been given. This step is completely separate and is absolutely necessary. It must be mastered before you can fully walk in God's supernatural provisions. After you have learned how to properly manage what you have, then you are ready to use your faith and expect to receive an increase in your resources.

Even if you have made every financial mistake that is possible, if you repent and start to operate under God's financial plan, God will honor your faith.

If you are in a situation in which you don't have enough money coming in to meet your financial needs, or you are caught in circumstances in which you are locked into the poverty cycle, first you must learn to be faithful with what you have. God can change financial circumstances, but you must take a step of faith (some action) for something else to come your way other than what you currently have. It will more than likely require extra effort on your part, but remember that the victory will only come to those who are willing to put forth the effort to overcome their situation.

RECEIVING GOD'S SUPERNATURAL INCREASE

And Pharaoh said unto Joseph, See, I have set thee over all the land of Egypt. And Pharaoh took off his ring from his hand, and put it upon Joseph's hand, and arrayed him in vestures of fine linen, and put a gold chain about his neck; And he made him to ride in the second chariot which he had; and they cried before him, Bow the knee: and he made him ruler over all the land of Egypt. And Pharaoh said unto Joseph, I am Pharaoh, and without thee shall no man lift up his hand or foot in all the land of Egypt.

Genesis 41:41-44

Joseph had nothing when he was taken to Egypt, not even the coat of many colors given to him by his father. But by being faithful with what he had been given and faithful to God's Word, he was able to change the economic destiny of an entire nation and walk in the supernatural provision God had destined for his life.

Joseph was a slave, but God blessed him in spite of his economic circumstances. The Bible states that Joseph was a successful man, and God blessed Potiphar's house for Joseph's sake:

And Joseph was brought down in Egypt; and Potiphar, an officer of Pharaoh, captain of the guard, an Egyptian, bought him of the hands of the Ishmeelites, which had brought him down thither. And the Lord was with Joseph, and he was a prosperous man; and he was in the house of his master the Egyptian. And his master saw that the Lord was with him, and that the Lord made all that he did to prosper in his hands.

Genesis 39:1-3

What was it about Joseph that made him so successful in spite of his difficult circumstances? What was it that Potiphar saw? What were the principles Joseph used that were so powerful they could change the economic destiny of an entire nation? What was it Joseph did that caused God to act on his behalf? What economic principles and biblical guidelines do we need to glean from these scriptures in order to get an understanding that will affect our economic heritage?

LOOKING PAST POVERTY TO PROSPERITY

God wants us prepared to receive supernatural increase. According to the Bible, the world conditions will get worse and worse. But as the world deteriorates, God will bless the church both spiritually and financially. He will raise up individuals within the local church who have been found faithful and trustworthy stewards in order to receive the wealth of the world to finance the end-time harvest.

The wealth of the sinner is laid up for the just.

Proverbs 13:22

Ye rich man, weep and howl for your miseries that shall come upon you. Your riches are corrupted...Your gold and silver cankered...Ye have heaped treasure together for the last days.

James 5:1-3

Just as in Joseph's day, many are slaves to the world economic system. They are held captive by myths, religious traditions and the wrong attitude about handling money. Many have made debt their master and overseer. They are in bondage to their jobs or the money it provides. They bow down and make a monthly pilgrimage to the god of instant credit (the credit card), often paying more in interest to the world's economic system than they give to God. Even if they wanted to do something for the kingdom of God, they wouldn't be able to because they are barely able to take care of themselves. They are locked in prison without realizing there is a way out.

God really wants us to prosper spiritually, mentally, physically and financially. God wants us to break the bondage in our lives so that we can become true stewards for Him. He wants us to become free so we can have an impact for the kingdom of God.

God wants to raise up stewards that He can trust to use their faith to receive supernatural increase. The increase is not merely to meet our needs, but to help meet the needs of others and to establish God's covenant in the earth for the end-time harvest of souls.

> *But thou shalt remember the Lord thy God: for it is He that giveth thee power to get wealth, that He may establish His covenant.*
>
> Deuteronomy 8:18

God has put within every individual the desire to do great things — the desire to help his fellow man, his race, his community and his nation.

God has given us all gifts, creative talents and ideas that could immediately change the financial circumstances of our lives. However, most people live unfulfilled lives. They think, "If only we had the money to develop our ideas." Yet Joseph, while he was in prison with no money, flourished like a flower.

> ### ACTION STEP:
> ### USE THE GIFTS AND TALENT
> ### GOD HAS ALREADY GIVEN YOU

Most people shut down the ideas and suppress the gifts God has given them because of their circumstances. "No money, no credit, born on the wrong side of the tracks," or any number of other obstacles seemingly beyond our control, keep us from fulfilling the creative desire God has instilled in us. Therefore desire dies on the vine and never comes to fruition! We never fulfill our purpose in life. We never walk in our inheritance.

In this chapter, we will take a close look at how to develop the creative ideas that God has given you. In Chapters 1-5, we looked at the fundamental principles in the Bible that show how to build a foundation to handle God's wealth and what to do with the resources once they have been entrusted to your care. Here we will look at faith for God's supernatural increase.

This section has been put last for a reason. If a person receives wealth without knowing how to handle it, it will disappear.

The Bible points this out through the Scriptures:

Wilt thou set thine eyes upon that which is not? For riches certainly make themselves wings; they fly away as an eagle toward heaven.

Proverbs 23:5

FAITH IS BEING
PREPARED TO RECEIVE

Keep your faith line in the water and prepare yourself to receive God's blessing. If you have already demonstrated your faithfulness in properly managing what you have, expect immediate results.

God has reminded me of some things about fishing. First of all, He reminded me that to catch a fish, you must have your "faith line" in the water. To catch a larger fish, you might even have to move to a larger pond (where the big fish are). You might have to launch farther out into the deep water.

You might have to prepare for a larger increase. You might have to get a larger boat and heavier equipment.

Most of all, you must be prepared to handle the big fish when you get him in the boat, or the fish could either sink your small boat or swallow you up. Joseph was prepared when his time came because he never stopped using the talent (gift) God had given him. He kept his faith line in the water.

Unless we cast your line into the water, we will not catch fish. Those who want to plug into God's supernatural blessings must prepare themselves to receive the blessings before they come. A proper foundation must be laid. We must learn and begin to practice the biblical principles that govern money.

ACTION STEP:
PREPARE TO RECEIVE YOUR BLESSING
BEFORE IT COMES

According to Luke 16:9, you should become the friend of the world's unrighteous money. Also Luke 16:12 asks if you're not faithful with another man's property, who will give you that which is your own?

And I say unto you, Make to yourselves friends of the mammon of unrighteousness; that, when ye fail, they may receive you into everlasting habitations.

Luke 16:9

And if ye have not been faithful in that which is another man's, who shall give you that which is your own?

Luke 16:12

You should already see the evidence of increase in your life. You should have become experienced by being a good manager of other people's property first. If you have been applying biblical principles of stewardship, you should be able to see the results of God's increase. Reread Chapters 1-6, which deal with the stewardship principle, planning and preparation, debt, honesty, integrity and giving.

ACTION STEP:
DEVELOP THE CREATIVE IDEA
GOD HAS GIVEN YOU

Prepare a written plan of action. Research the cost and income figures. How much will it take to produce the service or finished product? How much do you need to advertise and market the product or service.

ACTION STEP:
AFTER GOD GIVES YOU AN IDEA
BE WILLING TO CHANGE YOUR LIFESTYLE

Make sure your ideas are clear to you and that you can explain them clearly to others. There are opportunities all around you; it doesn't matter if the economy is going down or up. There is always room for creative ideas. But most opportunities are going to require action on your part. They may require that you change some old habits. You may have to get a second job, or even go back to school!

Keep your faith line in the water. While you develop a written plan, don't let Satan steal your idea or desire to see it fulfilled. Don't be discouraged by those who do not understand. Stay away from those who will dash cold water on your desires. Be willing to change your lifestyle.

```
ACTION STEP:
START WHERE YOU ARE AND
BE FAITHFUL WITH WHAT YOU HAVE
```

Don't develop any new bills or try to borrow money until you have tested your idea. Make sure there is a market for your idea. Use the money you have in your savings or the creative gift that God has already put inside you to develop the idea and a plan of action that is self-financing. If you have a good idea, it does not always take money.

```
ACTION STEP:
ASK GOD TO GIVE YOU
UNDERSTANDING OF HOW TO DO IT
```

I remember the first business I started. I only had the idea and the energy; someone else put up the money. I worked and provided the manpower; and we split the profit.

In the second business I started, God gave me an idea to market a new product. I developed the marketing concept and borrowed money to buy the first unit. I let the lender keep the product as collateral. When we sold the product, there was enough profit to pay the lender and buy new items for inventory that I owned 100%.

THE EXAMPLE OF JOSEPH

In analyzing the life of Joseph, there are several things that always stand out.

1. He never forgot the promise God had given him. He could see where he was headed based on God's promise (Word), not on the circumstances that held him captive.

2. Joseph made the most out of what he had. He played the hand he had been dealt. He acted on what God had given to him, no matter what his circumstances. He worked as if unto the Lord — he was obedient to God's holy calling.

3. He never forgot that he was a servant of the almighty God, even though he was in prison and in bondage to another man.

4. He used the gifts and abilities he had for the benefit of the person to whom he was serving as a slave, but he always gave glory to God for the gift.

5. He was a giver. He gave out of what he had. He never forsook his gift because he did not have money or freedom, nor when he was misused or treated unfairly. He blossomed where he was.

6. He shared his gift with whomever he came in contact, whether that person had money or not.

Because of his faithfulness with what he had been entrusted, Joseph was a man who could be trusted by God and man!

God knows the condition of the heart of man. He cannot operate to His fullest capacity in those who are not faithful with the finances He has already entrusted to their care.

As a steward, we must learn to follow the instruction that God has given us and not waste God's money. We must learn the true purpose of wealth in the lives of a Christian and be willing to be a co-worker with God to establish His covenant in the earth.

Yes, God still answers prayer, but He can only give true wealth to those who have prepared themselves in advance and know how to handle it. We must use our faith to develop the resources if we do not have money or wealth. It takes obedience to walk in the inheritance that God has set in place for us from the foundation of the world.

Remember, as stewards the resources with which God has entrusted us belong to God. They will be in our trust (care) only for a short period of time while we are here on earth. This does not mean that God does not want us to enjoy the benefits of them while we are here on earth, but He does not want us to consume them all on ourselves. He wants us to help Him establish His covenant here on earth. Again we should remember the principle God is clearly outlining in Deuteronomy 8:18:

> *But thou shalt remember the Lord thy God: for it is He that giveth thee power to get wealth, that He may establish His covenant which He sware unto thy fathers.*
>
> Deuteronomy 8:18

Jesus makes it even clearer as He discussed this matter with Peter in the tenth chapter of Mark:

> *And Jesus answered and said, Verily I say unto you, There is no man that hath left house [possessions], or brethren, or sisters, or father, or mother, or wife, or children, or lands [possessions], for my sake, and the gospel's, But he shall receive an hundredfold now in this time, houses [possessions] ... with persecutions [now, here on earth]; and in the world to come eternal life.*
>
> Mark 10:29-30

Jesus said, "an hundredfold now in this time," but the condition is for Jesus' sake and the Gospel.

As stewards, we must remember that all worldly wealth and material possessions will remain in the earth. It's what we do with what we have been entrusted here on earth that has an impact for Jesus and the kingdom of God. Only what we have done with what we have will benefit us when we get to heaven: How many souls did we impact for God? What did we do for the poor? Did we get the maximum benefit from what we had? Did we use our faith to do what we were instructed to do? Did we fulfill our purpose in life?

YOU MUST BE OBEDIENT: ACT ON YOUR ECONOMIC DESTINY

Now you must act on what you have learned! We have covered principles that have changed the lives and destinies of countless thousands. But knowledge alone will not get the job done. Now that you know that God has a financial system, you must be able to apply those principles to your life. You must act on what you have learned.

ACTION STEP:
ACT ON GOD'S FINANCIAL PLAN
TO CHANGE YOUR FINANCIAL CIRCUMSTANCES

In I Kings 17:8-16, we see the widow of Zarephath down to a cake and a handful of meal when Elijah, the prophet, came to her. She had almost nothing left. But because of her obedience and faithfulness to do what the Word of God said through Elijah, she had no lack and her needs were met.

If the widow had not obeyed the Word of the Lord spoken through Elijah, she would not have received the blessing God had for her. She and her son would have died for lack of food. Because of her obedience by acting on the Word of God, she enabled God to turn her whole situation from that of death to life!

Ask God in faith to show you what to do or how to use what you already have. Ask Him to give you a creative idea. God can change your circumstances, but you must be willing to act. You must put your faith line in the water and expect to land a financial blessing.

ACTION STEP:
REMEMBER THAT FAITH
WITHOUT ACTION IS DEAD

STARTING A BUSINESS TO
GENERATE ADDITIONAL INCOME

Ask God for a good business idea. One of the best ways to generate income is to identify something you would enjoy doing and use it to provide a service to others. This could be a hobby that you or someone you know has.

If you currently have a job working for someone else, examine the possibility of marketing the same service on an independent basis. The main idea is to identify a market to which you could supply a product or service.

A good place to start is to examine existing businesses that have been successful in your area of interest. Remember, the possibilities are unlimited. Ask the Lord to give you understanding of how to make your service or product valuable to other people. A good idea is to go by the library, and you will find many books and articles on how to start and develop a new business.

GET WISE COUNSEL

Call the Small Business Administration (SBA) office in your city and ask for information and assistance. The SBA's Service Core of Retired Executives (SCORE) often conducts seminars on various aspects of starting and building a small business. Another way to get good advice is to contact Christians who have businesses and experience in your area of interest.

PRACTICAL APPLICATION

One of the worst problems I have had as a businessman since I asked God for creative ideas has been a proper balance of time. After God gives you an idea for a business to break the economic bondage in your life, the devil tries to use the business to take your time with God.

I am listing below several points you should remember as God starts giving you creative ideas:

1. Keep your priorities straight. Give God the glory!

2. Give God your time.

3. Give God the credit. Let God be responsible for bringing in the money for the success of the business.

4. Allow God to give you the guidance to keep your priorities straight.

5. Be patient and content; cast your care on the Lord. Don't try to carry the load yourself.

HOW TO ACTIVATE YOUR FAITH

To receive God's supernatural increase, be faithful and apply faith to your financial circumstances. First, you must exercise your faith to believe it is possible for you to walk in the provisions outlined in the Scripture. Second, you must exercise faith to take the action steps necessary to apply the biblical principles to your financial circumstances.

To activate your faith, you must identify the scriptural promises that relate to your circumstances or conditions. Then, you must stand on these scriptures. Make them a part of you and a part of your daily devotion.

Listed below are scriptures that relate to financial increase. You should meditate on these scriptures daily. Put them on 3 x 5 cards and speak them out loud in the morning when you awaken and before you go to bed at night. Personal pronouns have been added to personalize the scriptures.

Use the scriptures listed below in conjunction with the "21 Practical Steps To Build Wealth In God's Economy" listed in Chapter 12. As you apply these action steps to your circumstances, you will begin to see the power of God start to work in your life to change your financial situation.

SCRIPTURES FOR FINANCIAL INCREASE

This book of the law shall not depart out of my mouth; but I shall meditate therein day and night, that I may observe to do according to all that is written therein: For then God shall make my way prosperous and then I shall have good success.

Joshua 1:8

I seek first the kingdom of God, and His righteousness; and all these things shall be added unto me.

Matthew 6:33

I shall remember the Lord, my God: for it is He that gives me power to get wealth, that He may establish His covenant which He swore unto my fathers.

Deuteronomy 8:18

The Lord desires above all things that I may prosper and be in health, even as my soul prospers.

3 John 2

The Lord has pleasure in the prosperity of me, His servant.

Psalm 35:27

My God shall supply all my needs according to His riches in glory by Christ Jesus.

Philippians 4:19

The Lord shall open unto me His good treasure, the heaven to give the rain unto my land in His season, and to bless all the works of my hand: and I shall lend unto many nations, and I shall not borrow. And the Lord shall make me the head, and not the tail; and I shall be above only, and I shall not be beneath if I harken unto the commandments of the Lord my God, to observe and to do them.

Deuteronomy 28:12-13

The Lord, my God, teaches me to profit, and leads me by the way that I should go.

Isaiah 48:17

I seek the Lord, so I shall not want any good thing.

Psalm 34:10

He that spared not His own Son, but delivered Him up for us all, shall also freely give me all things.

Romans 8:32

Christ has redeemed me from the curse of the law, being made a curse for me ... that the blessing of Abraham might come on me.

Galatians 3:13-14

God will go before me, and make the crooked places straight: He will break in pieces the gates of brass, and cut the bars of iron: and He will give me the treasures of darkness, and hidden riches of secret places

Isaiah 45:2-3.

I am willing and obedient, so I shall eat the good of the land.

Isaiah 1:19

I obey and serve God, so I shall spend my days in prosperity, and my years in pleasures.

Job 36:11

I know the grace of my Lord Jesus Christ, that He was rich, yet for my sake He became poor, that I through His poverty might be rich.

2 Corinthians 8:9

The wealth of the sinner is laid up for me, the just.

Proverbs 13:22

I am a faithful man, so I shall abound with blessings.

Proverbs 28:20

I delight myself in the Lord; and He shall give me the desires of my heart.

Psalm 37:4

God is doing exceeding abundantly above all that I ask or think, according to the power that works in me.

Ephesians 3:20

His divine power has given unto me all things that pertain unto life and godliness, through the knowledge of Him that has called me to glory and virtue.

2 Peter 1:3

I give, and it is given unto me; good measure, pressed down, and shaken together, and running over, shall men give unto me.

Luke 6:38

I am not slothful, but a follower of those who through faith and patience inherit the promises.

Hebrews 6:12

Jesus came that I might have life, and that I might have it more abundantly.

John 10:10

Jesus is my mediator of a better covenant which was established upon better promises.

Hebrews 8:6

I fear not, for it is my Father's good pleasure to give me the kingdom.

Luke 12:32

The blessings of the Lord make me rich, and He adds no sorrow to it.

Proverbs 10:22

*I do not grow weary in well doing, therefore in due season
I will reap because I faint not.*

Galatians 6:9

12

21 PRACTICAL STEPS TO BUILD WEALTH IN GOD'S ECONOMY

Even so faith, if it hath not works [corresponding actions], is dead, being alone. Yea, a man may say, Thou hast faith, and I have works: shew me thy faith without thy works, and I will shew thee my faith by my works [corresponding actions].

James 2:17-18

Be thou diligent to know the state of thy flocks [business affairs], and look well to thy herds. For riches are not for ever: and doth the crown endure to every generation?

Proverbs 27:23-24

To build wealth in God's economy, you must believe that it is possible for you to do what God says you can do and that you can have the financial resources that God says you can have. Then you must take action! Having financial surplus is the natural by-product of operating in God's financial system. It does not matter what your economic background or race is. As a steward, God expects you to use the ability that He has given you to manage and build resources. It doesn't matter where you start; it is where you end that counts. The starting point might be different for each individual, but God expects you to be a doer of the Word. He expects you to get started and be faithful in the process.

The secret to learning how to operate in God's financial system is to realize that you must do your part in order for

God to do His part. There are basic steps that should be taken by every individual who is interested in building a sound financial foundation and operating within the guidelines of God's financial system. The following 21 basic strategies incorporate the fundamental principles outlined in the Bible. They also summarize and incorporate all the ACTION STEPS listed in each chapter of this book. Every good financial plan will incorporate most, if not all, of these basic strategies. Use them as a checklist in organizing your financial plan.

STEP 1: WRITE OUT YOUR FINANCIAL GOALS

You must plan ahead to build wealth in God's financial system. First, tabulate your current financial condition to determine where you are, i.e., how much you own versus how much you owe. Second, from this financial statement, you should write out your financial goals, where you would like to be in the future (five, ten, even twenty years from now) your net worth, your income goals, your giving goals, your goals for saving and your goals for education (for you and your children). You also must make a realistic estimate of living expenses. Third, write out your retirement goals. You must determine how much money you will need to have invested to live comfortably off the interest. These are important to your long-range success. Keep them in a safe place and refine them every year in your family's annual planning meeting.

STEP 2: LIVE WITHIN YOUR MEANS

Control your spending by establishing a written budget. You can use your personal checking account for this purpose. Set up a payroll deduction plan with a goal of living on 70%. Have 30% taken off the top before accounting for any living expenses. Never spend more than you earn. Remember, if you spend less than you earn, you will always have a surplus. This is a bedrock decision that must be made on your part. This is where you must draw your line in the sand. No matter what you earn, you must establish this as a minimum goal. Note: Earning more is not the main issue at this point in organizing your financial plan! No matter how little or how much you earn, you must learn to live on less than you have coming in. We will deal with the issue of increase in Step 19. Getting an increase is simple after we get a revelation of this step. If you are not willing to settle the issue of spending less than you earn, the other steps in this plan won't have any significant impact in changing your financial circumstances.

STEP 3: START A SURPLUS ACCOUNT: SET ASIDE SOMETHING FROM EVERY PAYCHECK

To start a wealth-building program, it is necessary to establish a surplus account. You should set aside a portion of every dollar you receive. After God, you should pay yourself first! A good rule of thumb to establish in this regard is: Whenever you write out a check to your church, you should be able to set aside (at minimum) an equal amount for your savings. This establishes your surplus account. If you cannot start with 10%, take a step of faith to start setting aside something. This is another bedrock of your financial plan. If you don't make a firm commitment here, you will continually be at the mercy of your financial circumstances. Make a quality decision. Drive your stake in the ground. Make a decision to start. Set aside something, even if it is only one dollar a week until you can see better times.

STEP 4: SET UP A SHORT-TERM EMERGENCY ACCOUNT

When you start your savings, the first money goes toward your emergency account. This account should have enough money to cover three to six months' living expenses. Use the surplus funds from this account to convert to a longer-term savings account as your funds accumulate. This account can also be used to make short-term cash purchases to avoid long-term debt and interest payments.

STEP 5:   KEEP PROPER RECORDS

Your checking account is the easiest way to accomplish this. To move toward your financial goals, you must have an accurate picture of where you are to determine if you are on target. Open a free checking account with no monthly fee or service charges. Run your income through your checking account so you will have a record of your income and expenditures. To form an accurate budget picture, it is very important to maintain this record.

STEP 6:   GET OUT OF DEBT

Break the spirit of debt in your life. The best way to avoid the debt trap is to never allow yourself to get hooked. If you are already overextended, set a debt-reduction plan, with a goal to live debt free within three to five years, or with a maximum of 10% debt. Never purchase anything on your credit card unless you have the resources to pay it off in full at the end of every month. The only way to break the habit is to stop all credit purchases until you get free of debt (especially credit card debt). Then avoid putting yourself in a surety position ever again. Since principal and interest payments are the largest expense item for the average family, by eliminating these payments, the average family will automatically increase their disposable income by as much as one-third. This savings can be applied to their surplus account.

STEP 7:   LEARN HOW TO MAKE
MONEY WORK FOR YOU

Be familiar with how money works. It is important that you know the basic principles of investing and compound interest. Once you establish surplus funds, you must have a place to put them. You want to learn how to get the best return possible on your savings with the minimum amount of risk. If you do not have time, you should employ a good financial planner who will assist you in keeping on track. It is important that you keep your financial goals in sight. It also is important for you to know what it feels like to have money (surplus) in your savings account. Your overall investment strategy should be consistent with your written financial goals.

STEP 8: OPEN A NO-LOAD OR REAR-LOAD MUTUAL FUND

Pay either no commission or a low commission when establishing your long-term investment accounts. As funds accumulate, you can move them from your short-term emergency account to your long-term investment accounts. For diversification purposes, most families will have a number of mutual fund accounts, i.e., money market fund, bond fund and stock fund (or a combination of these funds).

STEP 9: ESTABLISH AN IRA (INDIVIDUAL RETIREMENT ACCOUNT)

Use a good family of mutual funds to open your IRA account. This will help you earn the highest return on your long-term investment account. If you have an employer retirement plan, you should set a goal to always take the maximum deduction allowed for matching retirement accounts. Some employers match one-to-one. Others match two-to-one, and some even match three-to-one for every dollar the employee puts into the account. There are very few investments that can produce a greater return than a well organized employer/employee retirement account.

STEP 10: USE MONEY MARKET ACCOUNTS TO EARN INTEREST ON CHECKING ACCOUNTS

Let money earn interest for your short-term emergency funds while in your checking account (or use an interest-bearing savings account with check-writing privileges). The interest rate on these accounts may vary depending on market circumstances. However, having a money market account always gives you immediate check-writing access to your short-term savings. In addition, you get interest income that would normally have been lost.

STEP 11: ELIMINATE ALL UNNECESSARY WASTE FROM CURRENT INCOME

Get the maximum benefit from every dollar entrusted to your care. You dictate where your money goes, not the circumstances. Your goal is to manage every dime. Avoid every situation that robs you of your money (i.e., penalties, interest, fines, fees, tickets, late payments, fast-talking sales-people). Always be on the lookout for ways to reduce expenses and cut costs from your monthly budget.

STEP 12: AVOID BUYING INSURANCE YOU MAY NOT NEED

You can save up to 80% on your life insurance if you buy term life insurance instead of whole life or universal life insurance. Invest the savings you receive into your mutual fund or IRA account. You can also increase your wealth-building account by saving 40% to 50% on your automobile insurance. Increase the deductible from $50 to $500 minimum on collision/comprehensive/liability insurance. Use your short-term emergency account to self insure up to the $500 minimum.

Avoid purchasing credit life, credit disability and extended warranties on credit purchases. Use your best judgment here. However, these are usually very expensive insurance policies that are always calculated heavily in favor of the insurance provider. Outside of principal and interest payments, insurance is one of the highest expense categories for the average family's budget. By eliminating unnecessary coverage on your life, auto, home and other iscellaneous insurance, many increase their disposable income by as much as 30%.

STEP 13: REDUCE OR ELIMINATE ALL EXISTING INTEREST PAYMENTS

Every dollar you spend on interest payments is money taken directly from your disposable income. It is gone forever! Every dollar you spend on interest is a dollar that you could have working for you if it were placed in your interest-bearing investment account.

Your goal is to live debt free or have a maximum of 10% debt. You can save 10% on existing credit card debt by refinancing cards that are currently at the 18% to 20% rate with the new lower interest rate. Pay all credit card debts at the end of the month in which the purchase is made to avoid interest payments altogether. (See Step 6.)

STEP 14: SAVE UP TO 50% ON THE COST OF AN AUTOMOBILE

When purchasing an automobile, you can save up to 50% if you buy a two-year-old automobile with low mileage and the same body style as the later models. Use this same principle when buying furniture. If you are just getting started as a young family, your main goal is to avoid debt (short- and long-term). Use the newspaper classified ads to find a good buy. (Don't be in a hurry!) Then pay cash!

STEP 15: SAVE 25% TO 45% ON HOME PURCHASES

Buy a house wholesale at courthouse auctions, VA or FHA repossessions or directly from bank repossession inventories, and your savings can be between 25% to 45%.

STEP 16: SAVE OVER 30% ON EXISTING HOME MORTGAGES

Refinance your house from a 30-year mortgage to a 15-year mortgage at lower interest rates. Depending on the interest rates at the time, you can cut your total interest payment by as much as one-third. You can save substantial interest payments on your existing 30-year mortgage by also setting up a biweekly payment plan. If you pay your mortgage every two weeks instead of once per month, you will eliminate 10 years of interest payments. For example, pay $400 every two weeks instead of $800 monthly. You can accomplish the same thing (and get the 10-year reduction) by making one extra monthly payment each year. (Make sure the extra payment goes directly to your principal. For more details, contact your Stewardship in Action — Small Group Study Course leader or your financial planner.

STEP 17: LEARN HOW TO REDUCE YOUR TAXES

You should become familiar with the tax system. The average family pays 35% to 45% in state and federal taxes (not including sales taxes). Most individuals can still make tax-deductible IRA contributions. Whenever possible, make the maximum contribution to your company retirement plan. There are many expenses considered legitimate deductions when a person owns a small business. You can invest in tax-free mutual funds. There are legitimate ways to reduce your tax expenses to receive a substantial savings in this area. Ask your financial planner for additional help in this area.

STEP 18: ESTABLISH A WORKABLE ESTATE PLAN FOR YOUR FAMILY

Prepare a will to avoid unnecessary court and probate costs. By establishing a workable estate plan, you can save on taxes and provide additional resources for your family.

STEP 19: LOOK FOR CREATIVE WAYS TO INCREASE CURRENT INCOME

Now that you realize that as a good steward you must live within your means, the next step is to use your faith to generate additional revenue. If you are not happy with your current income, it's time for a change in your lifestyle. Ask God for creative ideas to utilize your existing talents. Ask God to show you ways to make yourself valuable to someone else. Ask God to show you ways you can use what you have to produce more income. Ask him for specific things you can do starting from where you are. Identify a need in someone else's life and become a solution to that person's problem. Reread Chapter 11, "Faith for God's

Supernatural Increase." Just one creative idea from God can change your financial condition overnight.

STEP 20: PLANT A SEED TO HELP SOMEONE ELSE GET THEIR FINANCES UNDER CONTROL

Give of yourself in both time and money. After you begin to get your finances in order, look for an opportunity to help someone else. (Set aside a portion of your short-term savings specifically for this purpose.) You must be willing to share these principles with others who need a financial breakthrough in their lives (family, friends and business acquaintances.) The easiest way to share these principles is to invite them to attend the next 12-week Stewardship In Action — Small Group Study Course held in your area. If you don't have a Small Group Study Course in your area, ask your pastor if you can start one at your church.

STEP 21: BE PATIENT

The greatest hindrance preventing individuals from walking in God's financial system is the lack of patience. Now that you know what God's financial plan is, you must be willing to act on it. But financial freedom will not happen overnight. For the average family that has serious financial problems, it could take three to five years to get out of debt and turn their finances around. The great temptation will be to try to rush this process. Set your course, establish your plan and stick to it. The basics cannot be rushed. However, the time frame can be drastically reduced by adding faith to the equation. Give God an opportunity to work on your behalf.

For the average individual to apply these 21 steps to their financial circumstances, it will require a major change in lifestyle. Remember, you do not have to do these steps in your own strength. If you do your part, then you bring God on the scene, and He will do His part.

In addition to the action steps listed above, go back to Chapter 11 and review the scriptures on financial increase and draw strength from them. Ask God to give you the wisdom and understanding to be able to implement these steps as God makes them real to you.

My prayer for you is that God will give you a fresh and powerful revelation of the abundance that is available in His economic system and as you get your financial house in order, you will reach out to others and have an impact for the kingdom of God.

THE COMMITMENT

For those individuals who are serious about getting their financial house in order, we are asking you to make a firm commitment by filling in and signing the form below. Then make two copies. Place one in a prominent location to remind you of your commitment, and send the other copy to Urban Impact Ministries. We want to stand with you in your commitment and hear of your progress.

Dwight Nichols

I hereby commit this day _____ (date) to take the actions necessary to get my financial house in order, and to change the attitude and lifestyle that keeps me in financial bondage. I further commit:

1) To break the spirit of poverty in my life by using my faith to get out of debt and increase my earning capacity to have a greater impact for the kingdom of God.

2) To establish my surplus account by spending less money than I earn and saving something from every paycheck.

3) To become self-sufficient and avoid any form of long-term government assistance.

4) To make compound interest work for me instead of against me by opening a long-term savings account or an Individual Retirement Account (IRA) this year [or by _____ (date)].

5) I commit to help at least two other families get their financial houses in order by sharing these principles of financial freedom. (The best way to accomplish this is by inviting them to the next Stewardship In Action — Small Group Study Course in your area.)

In Jesus' name,

Signed: _____

(Please print)   Name: _____

Address: _____

_____

STEWARDSHIP IN ACTION —
SMALL GROUP STUDY COURSE

The principles outlined in this book are organized into a small group study course, which is being taught in churches and other institutions across the country. The small group study course is a valuable tool to support local churches in strengthening their congregations financially by teaching the principles of biblical stewardship.

If you would like more information on how to start a Stewardship in Action — Small Group Study Course in your area, write:

Dwight Nichols

P.O. Box 901

North Little Rock, Arkansas 72115

or call (501) 834-1168

(Dwight is also available to conduct workshops and seminars on the foundational principles of biblical stewardship and money management.)

Harrison House

Proclaiming the truth and power
Of the Gospel of Jesus Christ
With excellence;

Challenging Christians to
Live victoriously,
Grow spiritually,
Know God intimately.